The Podcaster Posse
Tracking Outlaw Supermayor Tiffany Henyard

I0022942

Haven Simmons

Table of Contents

Copyright

Published by Defiance Press & Publishing, LLC

Bulk orders of this book may be obtained by contacting Defiance Press & Publishing, LLC. www.defiancepress.com.

Defiance Press & Publishing, LLC

281-581-9300

info@defiancepress.com

DEDICATION

This book is dedicated to friends, and my parents who raised me in Cedar Rapids, Iowa, 253 miles from Dolton; to friends in Salisbury, Maryland, 789 miles from Dolton; to friends in Sarasota-Bradenton, Florida, 1,208 miles from Dolton; and to friends and family, especially my wife, in Eugene-Springfield, Oregon, 2,142 miles from Dolton.

PREFACE

My tawdry tale of Tiffany A. Henyard began when an old buddy of mine in Iowa, the "Frenchman," already disgusted by political imbecility and transgressions, told me about an unhinged mayor from Illinois. Thank you, as writing this book demanded timely immersion in the story. After zealously sifting through legacy media news clips and articles, I levitated to You tube platforms for additional digging and the visceral human need to be entertained that Henyard's audacious behavior provoked. My background in television, newspapers, and local government was only part of the reason I got hooked vicariously on the sordid saga. It was like watching a movie where justice and the good guys simply must prevail. I kept wondering, when will this maniacal criminal and her thugs meet their Napoleonic Waterloo? Residents and the content creators I encountered, also known as the Podcaster Posse for the purpose of this book, were instrumental along with a tenacious social activist in attracting public and media scrutiny of Henyard's rampage through the Village of Dolton and Thornton Township.

CHAPTER I: THE POSSE

Hurry, hurry, hurry, step right up to the greatest show on Earth!

That invitation pertained to the circus, of course, but could readily apply to the saga of self-proclaimed "Supermayor" Tiffany Henyard who presided lawlessly and notoriously over Thornton Township and the Village of Dolton, Illinois, for four years. Rivaling the sleaziest malice, avarice, and hucksterism, the travails of her crimes and shenanigans reached national and global proportions in this brave, new technological world because of social media, including our Podcaster Posse content creators intersecting with hundreds of thousands of viewers, subscribers, and one another to observe, analyze, and topple the object of their fascination.

The outrages of the mayor and her inner sanctum mesmerized information junkies joining the posse on cyberspace platforms such as Cooking With Frank (not to be confused with an actual cooking show of the same name), IamJ9eve, Hannibal Is Hungry, Just Doing Nails (unlike another site, it has nothing to do with manicures), Chawanne Burns, AG Tactical, News For Reasonable People, AK COLE, Actual Justice Warrior, Nate The Lawyer, Go Political and Mob Vlog, the nexus of this sordid journey along with social activist and independent investigative "boots on the ground" reporter Jedidah Brown.

"What's up y'all?"

"Smash them likes."

"Hit that Subscribe."

"It's that time again."

"Cookin' With Frank."

"Frank" introduces himself on every episode in a laid-back, conversational and soothing manner. It is somehow reassuring to his fans that "Frank" has not disappeared from orbit, remains on task with creative graphics like the smoking microphone from overheating, and vigilantly follows the developments surrounding Henyard, Thorton Township, and the Village of Dolton. She is HEN-yard, Hentard (presumably mocking retard), Hair Hat Tubman for her ludicrous comparisons, and Tim Henyard when he substitutes her hyena yapping with a contorted, deliberate male voice. As the program progresses, and with the drone of sultry music and discreet drumbeat, he alternates between agitation and hilarity with zero reverence for political correctness. Keeping with the cooking theme, "Frank" usually promises to come back and "chop it on up" after segments in the episode.

A terrific combination of entertaining and informative, as the first podcaster the author encountered researching Henyard, and his deference to other content creators deservedly earns Frank the mantle of Sheriff. Much like his peers, he admits to having never visited the community, a testimonial to the prevalence and influence of the medium.

Frank offers an "Adult comedy and reaction and reviews channel focusing on celebrities, musicians, athletes, politicians, comedians and more. Cooking With Frank provides a unique, comedic view and response to different topics such as relationships, sports, and media. From corrupt politicians to the latest celebrity gossip and scandals, Cooking With Frank delivers in a way that no other YouTube channel does. Due to the nature of some topics, this channel is for adults only."

Frank, who appears to be a bearded black male in his late 40s vaguely but cooly resembling Frankenstein with shades and a cigarette dangling from his mouth, presents a retrospective in video clips of Tiffany Henyard's beginnings as the mayor of Dolton where the average yearly income is $40,000:

"This is when Henyard was takin' over and you knew they was plannin' to steal everything and say they don't give a fuck, so this is kind of where it all started."

Dolton trustees Stanley Brown and Andrew Holmes, Henyard and her assistant, Fenia Dukes, and Deputy Police Chief Lewis Lacey are among the village employees exhilarating at a neighborhood block party.

Brown is boogying with an unidentified older woman, raising the mind-boggling ire of Frank: "Why is you hypin' this old lady up to do that shit? Heh. Heh. Man, this is ridiculous. Now you gonna double down on this shit (Brown gyrating on bended knees), huh Stanley? Look at this nigger. This man got to be 70-some years old."

Holmes is dancing more slowly: "There go Andrew. Now that more your speed, Andrew."

As for Mayor Henyard: "Look at Tiffany's little devilish ass. She eggin' this shit right along."

After exiting his black, unmarked car, the fully uniformed Lacey imbibes in boogie fever as well: "Lame ass Lewis Lacey. That nigger's the same height as he is wide. That nigger four feet tall and four feet wide," Frank snickers.

Several public works employees appear as well in vests: "She on the clock with some chicken in her hand shakin' it up. Man, get the fuck out of here. These are the times I don't feel sorry for Dolton."

Mayor Henyard, known for an extensive wig collection, huddles with several children at the event. "Tiffany got a little bit of air in that hair hat, you know what I'm sayin'? That was probably the first new hair hat. That's probably when she had 'thief' Freeman (citing village and township administrator Keith Freeman) charge thousands of dollars-worth of hair hats on the credit cards and shit. This one look like it got a little less air in it."

Frank's commentary prompts a deluge of compliments from the cyber gallery:

"Boy do I look forward to these videos. I just started laughing out loud watching and people around me probably think I'm crazy."

"bro you be killing me. Free Dolton!"

"No one comes for Tiffany harder than Frank and I'm here for it! You have me dying over here laughing. Keep up the good work."

"Broh, your opening rant was stronger than a McDonald's Sprite."

"You are a straight up comedian."

"I'm eating at Frank's."

The festivities are winding down when Trustee Stanley Brown starts sashaying up the street ahead of other revelers. "Look at Stanley. Man, that's embarrassing. Why do you keep doin' that shit?" Frank asks incredulously.

The less nimble Andrew Holmes also approaches the unnamed female senior citizen from behind. "Just gettin' it in. He'd hit that. I don't know whose grandmomma this is."

Frank concludes his take on the block party by saying, "The goin' was good for Tiffany Henyard. The people was dancin' in the streets. Eatin' barbecue. Eatin' chitlins. Eatin' chicken."

Earlier in the episode, Frank addresses the city's young public works superintendent whose rap music he had parodied. "He (the employee also known as Unk low down) called me fat or something. You're reachin' boy. I don't know where he got that from. My video got more views than your shit. You spent hours makin' that horse shit. Maybe he confusin' me with Keith Price (an encased Henyard devotee) or that nigger down there at the real late night bariatric center."

A follower chides: "don't mess with Unk low down, he'll tell Momma."

The rapper, Frank says, also wears a hair hat: "The texture of that shit look like crack house carpet."

Frank is undaunted by Henyard's henchmen: "Yeah, looks like some of them boys in the Village of Dolton don't like Frank that much. Heh. Heh. Heh. Yea, and that's alright y'all because I don't particularly like none of them niggers either."

Personal animosity toward podcasters could only have been triggered by computer sparring because they discharged critiques from afar without bona fide physical presence. The content creators on the internet rely upon meeting videos, cyber supposition, shared intel, and legacy media reports to fortify their forays.

At one regular meeting, Supermayor Tiffany Henyard showed up in attire emulating Nino Brown, drug kingpin from the 1991 "New Jack City" gangster film. She pranced around in her ensemble as DJ William Moore, a city employee famous for kowtowing to her every wish, played the song "Bitch Better Have My Money." She carried a stuffed dog replicating a scene from the movie when Brown battered an underling.

"What is she, Nino Brown?" trucking business owner Lawrence Gardner asked. "Anything she wants done, she gets them to harass you. If you are not doing what she say, if you are not doing how she's saying to do it, you are a problem."

According to Gardner, Henyard's henchmen pestered him for monetary contributions to her political coffers and, when he stopped acquiescing, they fabricated a story that alcohol was being sold on the premises and yanked his business license.

Frank frequently calls Henyard a hood rat, slang for someone who lives and exhibits attitudes of inner-city life thriving on danger, scandal and lawlessness.

The term sociopath also gained traction regarding Henyard, who grew up in Dolton, matriculated at a college in Chicago that no longer exists, was arrested for breaking into cars, ran a failed burger joint, and became a Dolton trustee before being elected mayor:

--Not understanding the difference between right and wrong

--Not respecting the feelings and emotions of others

--Constant lying and deception

--Being callous

--Manipulation

--Arrogance

--Impulsiveness

--Risky behavior

--Difficulty discerning the negative aspects of their conduct

--Violating the rights of others through dishonesty

In sum, she developed an odious reputation for not possessing a conscience.

Just Doing Nails reminds her audience that she is not a psychologist, but plays videos that illustrate the Supermayor's smugness, superiority complex, craving for turmoil, and total lack of empathy.

Viewers relate:

"Your definition of a sociopath is a great description of Nino Brown. I rest my case."

"Money does not change a person it only reveals who they really are"

"This was a great episode featuring the chaotic mess that is these 2 government offices held by this one sociopath. And the cronies that support her."

"I have said this many times that she is a sociopath 100%. The men that she has surrounded herself are Simps. She manipulates these fools easily, it's sad to watch."

"She is a professional liar."

"Rejuvenated after causing chaos just like nurse Ratchet in Cuckoo's nest."

"This is not a good person; this is not a good administration. I wanna feel sorry for her because I believe there are mental illnesses," independent investigative reporter Jedidiah Brown tells podcaster Hannibal Is Hungry. "Ignorance doesn't give you a pass from breaking the law."

Compassion for Henyard was unattainable. Her insults and imbecility, while entertaining, inflicted untold damage upon too many decent people, local government employees as well, working for viability, paying bills, and trying to plan their lives with hopes and dreams.

Podcaster IamJ9eve relates the instance of a deputy clerk unbowed by Henyard's bullying.

The attractive, composed young woman with proper diction, according to IamJ9eve as she airs the video, is harangued by the Supermayor for not providing the date on the agenda of the minutes she is reciting from a previous meeting, something that has never been required. Aris Montgomery's reading is rudely, repeatedly sabotaged. Furthermore, Henyard says, the minutes were not posted on the village website.

Montgomery: "We don't control the village website. Whatever is posted, we have no control over that."

Henyard: "Please take classes to do your job."

Montgomery: "I did."

Henyard: "At the end of the day, if you get communication to the public about something they need to know, please do that."

IamJ9eve: "All she did was point out the truth, bitch."

The deputy clerk corrects Henyard's contention that her office must record every official remark in meetings.

Accusing Montgomery of sarcasm, Henyard berates her to "please get your facts right. That don't make sense. You don't even know how to talk good."

"That's a double negative bitch," says Iam9eve, laughing uncontrollably and calling the Supermayor a walking contradiction.

Henyard: "You need to get your office in order. The clerk is nothin' but a court reporter."

IamJ9eve: "Can we see your (Supermayor's) college transcripts? Come on, man, what are we paying you for?"

"I'm the only one producin'," says Henyard, whose cackling arouses the same vibe as fingernails on a chalkboard.

Montgomery: "May I be recognized?"

Henyard: "Go ahead."

Montgomery: "I'm gonna make this very quick because you already wasted enough of the people's time."

With that, IamJ9eve is prepared to knight the deputy clerk, and more. "I would like to propose (singing as she goes); will you marry me? I don't have a ring, I'm sorry. Oh my God, I love this lady."

"I think you are looking for a transcriber," Montgomery asserts while challenging Tiff-Tiff to study the statute pertaining to minutes.

IamJ9eve says the deputy clerk deserves applause befitting Lady Gaga.

Henyard: "Y'all need to be respectful. Be respectful, deputy clerk."

Montgomery submits that she is respectful.

Henyard: "You outta order. People need to learn to stay in their place. Stop lying to the people. Y'all need to come to work. Y'all are never here."

Trustee Kiana Belcher retorts: "It's not fair that she treats us like kids."

Cooking With Frank rebukes the charlatan mayor: "She sat up there and ran off at the mouth again with the Bobby Brown bottom lip. I don't see why she would do her lipstick like that when it's higher on the bottom lip that accentuates that bottom lip, that keeps flappin' in the wind."

Belcher, once a member of the so-called Henyard "Dream Team," drastically lost patience with Henyard, earning kudos from IamJ9eve and other podcasters. IamJ9ever declares her a "hero" with the qualifier that she would probably succumb to high blood pressure and anxiety as the actual mayor.

Seeking revenge, Henyard instructed Administrator Keith Freeman to change the code on the door to the clerk's office, barring access. Then, IamJ9eve shows a video of two female police officers escorting the exiled, terminated deputy clerk out of Village Hall.

"They (the cops) know they doin' some dirty fuckin' work," the podcast host says. "She (the deputy clerk) like 'fuck these bitches. Would I do it again? Yeah, can we do it now?'"

Nearing the finish line of this episode, IamJ9eve applies wishful thinking:

"She (Montgomery) should get a job in a restaurant where Tiff goes and get a job in the kitchen."

Henyard's obsession with agenda items was sketchy and suspicious knowing that township Trustee Carmen Carlisle, a constant aggravation, said hers occasionally, mysteriously vanished before meetings commenced. The consummate professional, Henyard was fond of calling Carlisle, once a proponent, "Carliar."

It is quite possible the agenda omissions were retribution for her broaching duress over fiscal accountability, something Henyard loathed.

"Just give us an amount (being spent for various services and commitments). I think that would help with our discussion," Carlisle calmly pleaded to the Supermayor.

Henyard: "We didn't have a problem with giving you an amount, but this is when you have to follow the leader. The leader is a visionary."

Carlisle had worked as Henyard's assistant: "I was told by her to make sure she had two trips booked a month, nothing under three or four days."

Village of Dolton Clerk Alison Key could relate to the cryptic shell game Henyard played with agendas:

"Each month the village clerk submits minutes to go on the agenda. Each month my minutes are not put on the agenda to be approved by the board of trustees. Last week, I submitted four sets of minutes for four meetings we recently had. Why my minutes are not being put up, I do not understand."

Initially Jerry Jones and Darlene Gray Everett, who silently but staunchly stuck with the Supermayor until the bitter end, were her main allies at the township; Dolton trustees Andrew Holmes and Stanley Brown also colluded with her dutifully.

"If not now, when?" Jones asked. "We've got a young lady that has the potential to take this town to great heights. She's gonna be good for this community."

"I am the township," the Supermayor told constituents.

Never shy about her prowess, Henyard said: "God don't make no mistakes. He put the right person here that he knew was going to do the work and take the lashes and bear the strength to keep going and doing it all."

The heavenly intercession did not deter the Redeemed Church of God Resurrection Power Assembly, according to Black Enterprise, from suing the Henyard administration for not applying the municipal zoning code to plans for renovation and expansion.

"In all my years, I've never seen such a blatant disregard for an ordinance and religious civil rights," the pastor said. "Religious institutions are permitted in the area under the zoning code. Based on statements from employees, the mayor is calling the shots."

"Doing it all" apparently meant an expensive, self-immersed door-to-door adventure distributing water during an infernal Chicagoland heat wave, according to Actual Justice Warrior, that was immensely emblematic of her tenure.

"She's giving out cases of water that maybe cost $5 to $7 but she's doing it with two camera crews, paid for by the taxpayer, a full police escort that fills up two SUV's, all of them making crazy overtime, people from the fire department, and all the other agencies. So, she's spending hundreds of thousands of dollars on herself securing her own support while she's giving residents bottled water."

The Supermayor resided in a fantasy world of denial: "We got a whole surplus (of funds) when there's always been a deficit here. So, stop!"

A woman approached Trustee Stanley Brown as he was ambling through the Village Hall parking lot: "You cannot rightfully say that you vote for the people. You vote according to Tiffany's agenda. You're a great stepper, a smooth stepper Stan, but do the right thing. A lot of people are watching you."

In the political prime of her infantile intellect, Henyard thanked supporters for turning out in "drones" rather than droves at the polls, plausibly explaining her unfathomable success.

The soulless, heartless aspect of the Soooooooopermayor surfaced with Dr. Nakita Cloud, who began as her publicist and elevated to chief of staff, the mayor's right-hand woman. Cloud was traveling to see her ill father-in-law one weekend when she suffered a serious heart attack and needed hospitalization. Cloud's attempts to notify Henyard were for naught, but she did contact the mayor's security squad. Ultimately, Henyard told her the heart attack was a flimsy excuse for calling out of work—that she should have taken her blood pressure medicine.

Just Doing Nails is the unseen podcaster with a velvety voice. Precluding a mission statement, Just Doing Nails says Henyard's habit of publicly chastising people started when she was a trustee boisterously mauling the Village of Dolton communications director for not passing out fliers announcing a meeting.

"Isn't she just a delightful being? Such a pleasure to be around, so well-mannered, so nice," Just Doing Nails purrs sardonically.

Her viewers are not enamored of the Supermayor:

"She needs to get a copy of: 'Hooked on Manners'. She is sickening."

"The projection is strong on her when she calls others dramatic…and unlawful…and petty…and sneaky…"

"I want to know why she looks like she is about to fall asleep one second in these videos, she looks like she can't keep her eyes open!!?!! Then we see other videos where she is going off on these manic episodes that literally make no sense at all!"

"I wonder what her parents think of her behavior? I wonder if she was EVER told no when she was growing up."

"Delusional. Bottomless psychopathic behavior, her Followers are desperate."

"When getto gets a job!"

"She is so hypocritical I can't stand her."

"libary—oh my word, her command of the language, I axe you!"

"You know those wigs that Tiff-Tiff buys must cost a lot of money. She needs taxpayers' money to pay for her wigs and this is the way she does it. Not to mention buying her boyfriend a $95,000 car."

"She's a single mother that's her fault not theirs. She's got a blank check from the taxpayers. She thinks she can spend as much as she wants because she is the Supermayor."

Assessing Supermayor Henyard's appearance carries the caveat that it is clouded by contempt for the individual. Staying more detached, the 40yish black woman of medium height and build is reasonably attractive, in a wild-eyed sort of way. Depending upon taste, and the amount of face cake, some people might be tempted. In the same vein, her outfits as queen of the south Chicago suburbs ranged from outlandish to stylish in myriad vibrant colors reflecting a gaudy array of jewelry; flamboyantly formidable, rarely wearing the same thing twice with an unlimited budget. Her rotating wigs or hair hats, in Cooking With Frank's perspective, became signature fodder for the Podcaster Posse and residents on a trajectory to clip her wings.

Her clothing baffles Frank: "Did y'all like Tiffany's karate outfit? Apparently, that bitch is a black belt," comparing her to Shogun. On another occasion she wore a "formal, asymmetrical neck business office body con pencil dress."

Henyard's outbursts, showboating, and frenetic desire for the spotlight manifested the traits of a narcissist whose triumphant soiree in Dolton, with a poverty rate of 15%, cost $15,000:

"If somebody would have said Tiffany is a narcissist, this ice rink being called Just Ice so you can name it after your daughter (Justice) is literal, physical, tangible proof of your narcissism. You just told on yourself in the form of an ice rink," IamJ9eve says.

The rink, built at a cost ranging from $350,000 to $1 million according to cyber sources, and sans the approval of Dolton trustees, was supposed to be readily available to the public, but mainly accommodated shindigs enjoyed by the mayor and her insiders.

"We didn't want that million dollar ice rink that none of the citizens can take part of," resident Thelma Price said.

Observing a video at the skating rink, IamJ9eve calls Henyard's daughter "adorable" and "I almost felt guilty talkin' shit about her mother."

Then she notes how far away the two will be from each other when the Supermayor is behind bars. "Just an ego. The ego on this one. I can't stand this woman. She's broken on the inside."

Henyard's derangement not only put her at odds with You tube podcasters and legacy media but cued self-righteous rebellion: "You keep telling your fiction. Fake stories. Fake news. I am basically fighting against the devil, the evil spirit. I'm the good spirit."

Enraged by a reporter and eschewing her own accountability, Henyard sent a scathing letter to FOX 32 Chicago alleging conflict of interest; continuous racial and misogynistic coverage of her, Dolton, and Thornton Township; engaging in a malicious smear campaign; producing false and defamatory accusations toward her and staff in a blatantly erroneous manner; subjecting FOX 32 and other media sources to liability; and violating the ethics of FOX 32.

Her ascent to Dolton mayor and supervisor of Thornton Township was apparently facilitated by mercurial madness, a generous portion of luck, and the fact there is no provision against holding both positions concurrently.

Essence featured Henyard in the article, "It's About Generational Change: Meet the Woman Who Became the Youngest And First Black Mayor Of A Chicagoland Town."

"For any Black girl that wants to get into politics and make a huge impact for your people, you can do it. Don't ever give up because anything is possible," Henyard told the New York magazine "directed at upscale African American women."

The online outlet Black Woman wrote, "America is a country that has been predominantly run by white men since its independence from Britain. There have been small changes to this long tradition as more inclusive efforts have been made to diversify leadership roles in politics. Tiffany Henyard has etched her name in stone in America's list of trailblazers."

Initially learning the ropes as a trustee, the Democrat narrowly won the mayoral Democrat primary race in 2021 over the incumbent, who had suffered a stroke and, paradoxically, fellow trustee Andrew Holmes. She swamped policeman Ronald Burge, Sr. in the general election, garnering 81% of the vote. Residents in the overwhelmingly blue state had certified their preference. The 37-year-old Henyard canvassed the neighborhoods engaging constituents. Her fiery trustee persona did not sufficiently signal what would transpire once she seized power, although a scurrilous gas giveaway on the stump stirred controversy. She was a meteor of energetic hope surrounded by a "Dream Team" entailing trustees House and Belcher, eventual foes impeding re-election, along with Alison Key, the village clerk. The community later learned why "politics makes strange bedfellows" is a reliable adage, and that lightning really does strike twice as proven by the self-puffing "Supermayor's" fusion of two jobs.

15

An agitated, newly minted Henyard interrupted Key while she was calling the roll, a task assigned to the clerk. "Did I call the roll? I'm still speaking. Like stop! Everybody wanna run stuff."

Key listed 32 purportedly ignored records requests in her lawsuit against Mayor Henyard, claiming that Administrator Keith Freeman said employees discussing any lack of transparency would be fired.

"She (Henyard) is a small child," Key said. "I am not gonna argue with a child," adding that she already has grandchildren.

Podcaster Just Doing Nails concurs:

"Tiffany Henyard, to me, is nothin' but a child who does whatever she wants, has no regard for others, doesn't follow any rules, and everyone else is just a casualty of war."

Thornton Township Supervisor Henyard personally berated the local school board after a Fourth of July event at Thornridge High School in Dolton was canceled because of ongoing construction.

An ugly scenario unfolded, prompting Dr. Nakita Cloud, who became a public relations specialist with the school system, to text message Keith Price, a Henyard heavy and the food pantry director for the township:

"President Nina Graham has requested that neither you nor Tiffany contact her phone. Any official business can be done via email. She expressed concern that the recorded phone conversation was a breach of her privacy and found the tone from Tiffany and now the text from you threatening. It's clear that the call originated from your side, and she asked that you cease any further contact and harassment."

Early in Henyard's mayoral reign, residents lined up for several hours outside the municipal courthouse following a deluge of $500 parking tickets levied by Dolton police that doubled when payments were tardy.

"At first I thought it was $50 and then I had to put my glasses on," Elizabeth Watson said, adding the cost was "not for a senior citizen on a fixed income."

Some of the citations were circulated on vehicle windows, while others arrived in the mail based upon surveillance photos of license plates.

"The outrageous amount is insane," another resident said.

Longtime Thornton Township Supervisor Frank Zuccarelli died at the age of 70 in January 2022 before his final term expired. The township, serving 17 villages including Dolton, was required to fill the position pending board approval within 60 days. After haggling and confusion over half-a-dozen meetings and pondering at least eight potential appointees with the deadline approaching midnight, trustees selected Tiffany A. Henyard to the supervisor's role commanding an annual salary pushing $250,000. Coupled with her profiteering at the Village of Dolton, she was suddenly making approximately $300,000. Trustee Christopher Gonzalez, a future nemesis, was the one who nominated her.

The township board's decision elicited "Whhhooooooooohoo" from Henyard as she raced ecstatically toward the front of the room. "I never saw this comin'!" Varied reactions peppered the audience as a distinct, incredibly prophetic voice was heard saying, "Y'all making a mockery of this."

Well-wisher Donkor Parker was over the moon: "Put your hands together for your new township supervisor Tiffany Henyard!"

Retrospective internet gadflies were less smitten:

"She ran up there like she won some money on a game show (because in her mind she did)"

"The concern on some of their faces is very telling"

"There goes the neighborhood"

"The 'price is right' contestant"

"Is this like the 2008 NFL draft when the Raiders drafted that quarterback (JaMarcus) Russell"

"That (appointment) means I'm totally blessed and everyone loves me," the juvenile Henyard exclaimed.

The Chicago Tribune editorialized about excess inherited and exacerbated by a Henyard juggernaut awash in frivolity:

"Bloated salaries are a huge concern in Thornton Township. After nearly three decades at the helm of the state's largest township, Zuccarelli padded his annual compensation to nearly $250,000. With the top dog pulling in that much, others in the organization collect paychecks that seem commensurate to the chief executive's compensation. For example, Jerry Weems, executive director of transitional operations, is on pace to gross $212,375 in 2022. The evening's moderator was Stanley Brown, who is set to get paid $66,465 this year as manager of a lawn mowing service. Dolton Mayor Tiffany Henyard, who succeeded Zuccarelli as township supervisor, recently appointed Brown to Dolton's Police and Fire Commission. The appointment is disputed because Henyard acted without consent of the Dolton Village Board. Brown's wife, Marcia Walker-Brown, is on pace to collect $58,470 this year as manager of a township lunch program for senior citizens. Ruby Donahue of Harvey, a longtime member of the township's Human Relations Commission, said she was concerned about how trustees picked Henyard to replace Zuccarelli. Donahue said she was dismayed by how Henyard was using taxpayer funds to stage social events. Henyard staged an elaborate swearing-in ceremony at the township hall, even though she already took the oath office a month ago. It looked more like a coronation of a queen than the inauguration of a public servant. The first song a DJ played was the 1980 Kool and the Gang hit 'Celebration.' Henyard seems to have elevated event planners, stylists, graphic artists and image consultants to inner-circle positions that Zuccarelli reserved for human resources coordinators and public access personnel."

Stephanie Wiedeman, executive assistant under Zuccarelli, was axed when Henyard snatched the reins. "Everything she has initially done has been to promote her, to get her name in households, to get people to buy into voting," said Wiedeman, who would eventually be essential to scuttling the Supermayor.

Also handed a pink slip at Henyard's inaugural meeting was Director of Human Resources Jennifer Jones.

Shortly thereafter, photographer Nate Fields met the same fate. Fields, an emotional celebrant for Henyard, was a township employee for nearly 14 years. Henyard had told him "Nate, whatever you need, I got you" when Zuccarelli passed away. Worse yet, Fields was physically accosted following a meeting by Henyard's boyfriend for being defiant.

Employees started dropping like flies. Job openings were posted on the village website without substantive descriptions, including marketing manager, staff photographer, executive assistant, social media team, public relations manager, municipal communications coordinator, senior communications coordinator, youth communications coordinator, special events manager, township editor, and event planner.

Henyard canned Samysha Williams, who worked in code enforcement and the building department between 2019 and 2022.

"I am disgruntled by how the administration treated the employees, the residents, the business owners, and even the contractors. No one should walk into a government office with questions and concerns and walk away feeling defeated," Williams said. "We were told as department heads several times on a daily basis not to help this person or that person because of personal issues."

More bizarre and ominous was the decision to lock Assessor Cassandra Elston out of her office. Elston, a meticulous public servant praised for community outreach, was elected by the people and did not theoretically take directives from the mayor. Even so, sensitive assessor's files were sprawled openly in a common area of the building while Henyard's goons, at the direction of Administrator Keith Freeman, commissioned her to a cubicle for fuzzy "dereliction of duties."

Trustee Gonzalez asked for an explanation.

"I did not lock her out of her office," Henyard said before addressing an abnormally large throng of media gaining interest in her bombast and chicanery. "You guys do not come here for anything positive in the township that has been done."

Gonzalez admitted that he felt uneasy the night Henyard was empowered when she went to Zuccarelli's office, propped her feet onto the desk of the deceased predecessor, and gloated over what troublesome trustees in Dolton would have to say.

The concept of a township is probably foreign to many people peripherally familiar with local government, but Thornton (population nearing 190,000) layers between enormous Cook County and the Village of Dolton (population 22,000). Henyard bloated herself to the steward of 18 jurisdictions even though the respective mayors retain a significant degree of autonomy.

The village and township inhabit the Chicago Southland, a contemporary term for an expanse comprised of 2.5 million people. The overwhelming majority live along Interstate 57, east to the Bishop Ford Expressway and the Indiana border. The south suburbs claim the highest rate of black homeownership in the country, and they are also struggling.

Crime is prone to being worse than in other Chicago suburbs. The enclave of Harvey reported 23 homicides in one year.

White flight from Chicago increased incoming residents following World War II, with south side Windy City blacks following suit. Heavy industry, steel mills, and railroads brought blue-collar jobs to the area, now yielding to a service-oriented economy. Among the prime attractions are the CN railway's American headquarters, the Ford automotive plant, the Credit Union 1 Amphitheatre, SeatGeek Stadium, and Wind Creek Chicago Southland Hotel and Casino.

Bo Kemp, the CEO of the Southland nonprofit Southland Development Authority, hopefully enumerated the challenges the area must navigate to flourish in the future:

"For decades, the south suburbs have suffered population loss due to several factors—manufacturing decline, white flight, increasing tax burdens and, now, retiring baby boomers. Population loss creates unbalanced tax burdens, drives commercial decline and leads to under-resourced municipalities with insufficient funding to meet their needs or maintain existing infrastructure.

The manufacturing development post-WWII was a major pull for Black Southerners to Chicagoland. This could easily become a push in a decade if we continue to price Black families out of the marketplace.

We are at an inflection point. But I'm confident we can stem future Black-out migration. The 2030s and beyond will see significant population growth in the southland region, due to climate migration and the attraction of our redeveloped infrastructure and diverse workforce.

An increasing middle-class workforce is a lagging indicator of regional success, yet a declining one is a leading indicator of future regional woes. Without planning, this coming growth will have the unintended consequence of shrinking the ability for middle class workers to live in proximity to the quantum computing and AI jobs, the restaurants and retail opportunities, and the advanced manufacturing positions anticipated to power the state in the coming decades. We risk pricing workers out of the region and possibly the state.

Growth in the south suburbs will allow for a growing middle class to live and work in the Chicagoland region and support the state's efforts to attract future-forward industries. As the south suburbs go, so goes Chicagoland and the state of Illinois."

Sadly, hope did not spring eternal for Henyard's victims.

CHAPTER II: TIFFANY MOST WANTED

In a moment drooling with deception as she established her domain in Chicagoland, the Supermayor introduced herself to Village of Dolton residents by clumsily stating: "I am not for the taxpayer dollars for doing personal things."

As many aghast people would confirm, the honeymoon with the burgeoning governance of Tiff-Tiff, as she was uncharitably labeled, did not last long. The Soooooopermayor (her screeching words on countless occasions) soon faced intense scrutiny of travel to Las Vegas, Atlanta, Portland, Austin, New York City, and Washington, D.C. on the township taxpayers' nickel. First class airfares, 5-star hotels, and the best restaurants accrued credit card charges surpassing $100,000.

The Las Vegas excursion treated the Supermayor, Dolton Trustee Andrew Holmes, two administrative assistants, two township trustees, two Dolton police officers, and a photographer to top-shelf accommodations. The fateful trip also resulted in allegations that Holmes sexually assaulted one of the assistants, Fenia Dukes, a trusted Henyard supporter and friend.

The supposed purpose of the Las Vegas venture was to attend the International Conference of Shopping Centers in hopes of connecting retailers and communities for projects, something Village of Homewood Mayor Rich Hofeld questioned. "I am not aware they (Thornton Township) have an economic development leader, committee or anything like that. (Henyard's) way of doing business is not the way we do things. She's an embarrassment to local government."

Illinois law, incidentally, stipulates three basic township functions: road maintenance, property assessment, and "general assistance" comprised of food pantries and social gatherings, normally for senior citizens.

Around $11,000 was reportedly spent at the Fairmont Hotel in Austin, where Henyard claimed an (unnamed) conference had taken place. Cooking With Frank says that five people were gone for five days, even wasting public bling at a sports riding apparel store. Skeptical about the conference, Frank asks: "Why would they need to talk to the most ghetto mayor in America?"

Henyard and Administrator Keith Freeman attended the U.S. Conference of Mayors in Washington, D.C., the same week that he filed for bankruptcy protection. But the primary incentive for going was likely the photograph of President Biden and her beaming from ear to ear at a speech he delivered. Despite taking the trip in the capacity of mayor, more than $9,000 was charged to the township.

"That's one of the reasons I vote no when we go through our board packets," Trustee Chris Gonzalez said. "Some of the stuff, you don't know exactly what it's for and when you ask a question, there's no answer."

Planet Hollywood, Four Seasons Hotel, and the Marriott Marquis in Times Square also contributed to the fiscal doldrums of township residents, interspersed with high-dollar consumption for the palate at Ruth's Chris Steakhouse and other establishments on the various junkets.

Dr. Nakita Cloud criticized the Supermayor's extravagance. "Over the top meals! Lobster, crab legs, she likes the good stuff."

The Whitley public relations firm issued a statement defending the trips, sheepishly saying "they involved large groups crucial to building relationships, attracting investments and securing important development resources."

Auditors hired to evaluate the Village of Dolton's fiscal status were unable to render full accounting because of shoddy, delinquent records that camouflaged what was really happening. It probably did not help that Robert Hunt, a shrinking, cowering Henyard minion, was the village financial director humiliated in a meeting by the impatient Supermayor: "Make your comment Robert and go sit down!"

Henyard and Hunt earned the nickname "The Dynamic Duo" from Just Doing Nails for their seemingly unshakeable rapport as Dolton trustees in the past.

Her hand caught in the cookie jar did not hinder the unrepentant Henyard from dodging a television reporter's questions about squandering government funds recklessly in Las Vegas with a sly, cagey smile.

Tiff-Tiff: "I don't handle anything as it relates to credit cards."

23

Reporter: "Some of those charges are for you, though."

Tiff-Tiff: "No sir."

Reporter: "You didn't go to Las Vegas?"

Tiff-Tiff: "Ung."

Reporter: "You didn't go to Las Vegas?"

Tiff-Tiff: "No comment."

Reporter: "You don't know if you were in Las Vegas?"

Tiff-Tiff: "Of course I do."

Reporter: "Did you fly first class to Las Vegas?"

Tiff-Tiff: "Any other questions?"

Resident Sherry Britton confessed buyer's remorse concerning Henyard, doubting the Supermayor's stability and making comparisons to rapper Kanye West: "It was a vote that I regret deeply. When she got into office she just shut everyone out and went into the opposite direction. She became this tyrant and dictator."

She continued: "It seems like her aspirations and goals are to be a reality star. She didn't (previously) wear all that makeup. I don't know this for sure, but they say she is filming a reality show, because the cameras are always with her."

"I'm proud to announce the launch of the new Go Political channel. In this video, I give you an overview of the content that will be coming your way! I'm going to be talking about political discord in the US, and how our 2-party system has CULT CONTROL over its followers. Tired of biased propaganda coming from the news? Join me as I break down current events, and decipher what is REALLY going on in this country and the psychology of WHY we are experiencing such crazy developments in our society today. Buckle your seat belt because it will be a wild ride. Please like, subscribe, and tell a few friends!"

Crazy is the byword, according to video clips of a meeting on Go Political, when the Supermayor sanctimoniously says "I've always spent my own money for events" while aggressively debasing the relatively nominal expenses accrued by several Village of Dolton trustees and Clerk Alison Key at a conference in downtown Chicago, parking garage fees, and complaining that hotels can be found in the pricey Loop for under $200 a night.

Her prattling inevitably starts sentences with "As relates to," and unleashes barbs such as "the job (trustees) do is nothin'," and they should not be paid for their positions. The braggart, conversely, brings sponsorships and donations to the village.

Listeners, having heard music appropriately reminiscent of the original "Mission Impossible" show at the beginning of the podcast, are in no mood for Henyard's antics:

"Imagine living with this type of germ"

"Sounds like she is projecting her own LIE items!"

"Listening to Tiff talk is like watching someone fall down stairs"

"Narcissists are maddening! Thankfully Tiff is not smart enough to pull off any of the nasty tricks in the playbook without getting caught."

Trustee Ed Steave rebuttals Henyard:

"Stop saying 'if y'all don't know.' You were a trustee for eight years. You did the same for eight years. How do you wonderfully forget this stuff? You keep throwing out these disrespectful shots at everyone. You gotta stop that. It will never work with the tone you are taking right now."

Expectations for deflating the Supermayor's balloon were grounded with an unsuccessful recall attempt in the spring of 2022. Cook County Circuit Judge Paul Karkula ruled the referendum, spearheaded by the trustees' attorney, Burt Odelson, was unwarranted because of convoluted wording and the fact residents should have sanctioned holding a recall in the first place. The residents, wrongly bypassed in the process according to the judge, voted 1,960 "yes" and 1,536 "no" to oust the mayor, implying that community sentiments at the time still made her politically potent. An appeals court agreed with Karkula's decision.

"RECALL NULL AND VOID/I AM YOUR FOREVER MAYOR/I AM FOREVER AND WILL BE DOLTON'S MAYOR" signs appeared around the community in the aftermath as she adopted "Ain't No Stoppin' Us Now," a rousing anthem to her success that haunted the opposition.

Dressed for Christmas, Henyard's spew was spirited:

"I don't think any elected official should ever be recalled for this, especially when they ain't done anything wrong as relates to corruption, theft, brivery (presumably bribery), kickbacks, or anything."

"I just want people to understand I'm happy, leave me alone," said the embattled government matriarch whose swath of private lawyers over the years included dapper, unlicensed Max Solomon, accused of misappropriating revenue from a home foreclosure.

The desire to be left alone was inconsequential to her prolific parties, celebrations, and special events. "A Taste of Thornton Township" was superficially free but cost taxpayers more than $85,000, with a total of $50,000 paid to R&B singer Keke Wyatt and rapper J. Holiday for respective 30-minutes performances. The price tag for children's inflatable bounce houses was $6,600.

Once a Dolton trustee, Valeria Stubbs called the event a "flop," and estimated that 60 to 70 people attended.

"I was flabbergasted," said Jennifer Robertz, a township Village of Lansing resident. "I was pissed off. That's my money. That's the people's money."

The Supermayor was undaunted while preening on camera at the venue like a celebrity: "This is all for the babies. They don't show you this side of Tiffany Henyard: the productivity."

Trustee Chris Gonzalez said "A Taste of Thornton Township" received contracts before the board nixed bankrolling Gospel Fest, Home Fest, and several bingo bashes. "An extraordinary amount of money was spent unnecessarily. We can't continue to spend money without an (approved) budget) in place."

"You guys just halt things here at Thornton Township, because I don't see y'all doing nothin'," Henyard countered. "But yet, y'all started saying 'no' to everything myself and our team is coming up with and I see no ideas from any of you."

"I tried to stay away from the money," Henyard's mayoral forerunner Riley Rogers said. "It's not your money, so you can't use it like it's your piggy bank."

In her trustee role, the incubating dictator lectured Mayor Rogers on the importance of a mutual process: "You (the mayor) cannot pay a bill 'cause you choose to. The entire body have agreed not to pay that one particular vendor. What I'm asking as a trustee is that you report to your board. That's the structure, that's the order that you ignore every time."

The village owed Mosca Design of North Carolina $20,000 for unpaid banners and holiday decorations. A company official called it "very frustrating. This is something we did based on (Henyard) calling, being so excited. Just took her word for it and the signed documents."

Content creator News For Reasonable People ponders the latest hubbub in the Village of Dolton and Thornton Township:

"They (Keke Wyatt and J. Holiday) were big names at one point in time in their careers which was like 20 years ago, uh, 15 years ago. They got paid some pretty big money," he says. "This is a township and this is a village that is hemorrhaging money. You've just got these optics that are incredible. You're just like 'What—we're doing what? How does that work?' You bring in an artist and pay all this money and make it look like a re-election campaign."

His remarks induce an avalanche of listener feedback:

"The residents of the Village of Dolton are a disappointment to villagers worldwide. At this point in the movies the villagers using pitchforks and torches have cornered the evil monster in a burning windmill. Grow a pair Dolton!"

"I really love your commentary. Thank you for sharing the village of Dolton and Thornton Township story with your viewers. Jennifer Robertz"

"250 years ago, John Adams warned a young America that: America will get the government it deserves!"

"California is missing 11 billion of homeless funds"

"Henyard is doing her version of scorched earth."

"She gets better and better. Her ego isn't going to give it up until the handcuffs are on."

"I grew up in Harvey right next door to Dolton. I was always in Dolton for events, visiting friends that I went to high school with at Thornton Township High School. This was in the late 70s. A wonderful town. I am glad you are covering this. Love your videos."

"Why? WHY do they hire incompetent people? Voting on DEI vs. merit & ability will 'bite you in the butt' every time! Please PLEASE become an informed voter, it's your money"

"This has been going on for years, no one can touch her because she checks all the boxes. Anyone even tries, she screams that she is being discriminated against, and the accusers flee in terror spouting apologies for disturbing her important work."

Tightening her delusional stranglehold, Henyard invoked the race card to scold Dolton trustees for degrading her authority and authenticity. "You forget I'm the leader. Y'all should be ashamed of yourselves because y'all are black. Y'all are black! And y'all's sitting up here beating and attacking a black woman that in power. Y'all should be ashamed of yourselves."

For the record, 92 percent of Dolton is black, plenty of whom believed that the "Dictator of Dolton" moniker for Tiffany A. Henyard was compelling and not racially charged. In fact, they were appalled that Henyard compared herself to the likes of the iconic Martin Luther King, Jr., and abolitionist and women's suffrage activist Harriet Tubman, as a beacon for black Americans.

"The minute I took over—of course I'm black, young, and female—everyone wanted to attack," bellowed Henyard when her request for a referendum on a proposed mental health project was denied. She then eviscerated citizens ala Malcolm X for being "hoodwinked, bamboozled, and led astray" by board members worried that funds could be mishandled.

"The residents have spoken, and they've said they do not want your plans for a mental health facility, madam supervisor," Gartis Watts of South Holland village said. "It was voted down last Tuesday and there ain't nothing you can do about it. What happened to the mental health facility that was at the Riverdale site? If you're really concerned with mental health, start with re-staffing the mental health program the township already had."

The discussion occurred as an increasing number of people questioned the Supermayor's sanity and acuity.

"I ran to lead. You guys keep telling me what to do. We not going to do that," Henyard blundered in a typically illiterate gaffe.

"This should make up for all the bullshit she has done, you know? Keep that in mind," Cooking With Frank says referencing a back-to-school event hosted by Henyard.

Her gratuitous greeting to children is recorded at the site of a would-be police station and community hall, with a $50,000 sign installed at Henyard's insistence, that was never completed. Henyard had admonished

Trustee Tammie Brown for requesting an appraisal of the city-owned property comprising the Melanie Fitness Center that was losing money.

"It's your Supermayor, Tiffany A. Henyard, the people's mayor, and the people's supervisor. Everything's free, free, free, free, free! When you come to one of Tiffany Henyard's productions, it's free."

With marginal attendance, to no avail Cooking With Frank looks for two of his least favorite Henyard goons on the video.

"We ain't seen lame ass Lewis Lacey. He usually show his fat ass, don't he? Belly hangin' over his ass, all hyped up in the air with a little ass baseball cap and a big ass jersey. Like just his hands are stickin' out at the end of the sleeve. Can't even see that nigger elbow or nothin'—little pudgy, portly nigger."

"We didn't get to see Keith Price, the real-life niggapotamus. That nigger like three people sharing the two arms and two legs."

The Supermayor presses on for anyone willing to listen:

"I am so family oriented. I care about the youth. This is what they don't tell you or show you. I don't care about all the haters! You got to lead with love! There's so much hate that it don't make no sense. But I want to see their Supermayor still standin' after all their controversy."

Cooking With Frank also lampoons the Labor Day Weekend Exchange, an opportunity for Henyard and the rotund Price to present famished residents free boxes of greens, yams, canned goods, butter, turkeys and hams.

Price says that none of the goods are from the Chicago Food Depository while lionizing the Supermayor's generosity.

Frank: "You need to prove it's not from the depository. Shut your sloppy ass, Keith." Frank superimposes a head shot of Price with nothing but a humungous belly, punctuated by an "I'm fat" graphic.

According to Frank, her lover Kamal "Leotis" Woods is "a black version of pennywise the clown," and "that whole little area (Thorton Township and the Village of Dolton) is being ran by a bunch of punks—just punks, man—criminals just stealing from the people."

Cooking With Frank squelches conjecture that Henyard might seek refuge from the fray: "Where could Tiffany Henyard go to on the planet Earth to hide? That bitch could go to India. Soon as she cross the border, 'come and get this bitch please,'" Frank says with funky foreign intonation.

In addition, the host is intolerant of Henyard palooka Stanley Brown for voting against selling the vacant building where the celebration was held for the new school year: "This is a liquidation, nigger. Y'all need money in the bank!"

Regarding the Podcaster Posse in pursuit of Henyard: "The other content creators gonna keep it up, too."

Behold and tremble, peasants, would be an accurate depiction of the conniving, scornful Supermayor. "You outta order! You outta order!" she frequently screamed from her throne at startled residents. "Remove her! Remove him!" Nauseatingly demeaning was "Lemme educate y'all," as though trustees and citizens were empty vessels. Her opponents were accused of "politricks." The fatigued clichés "At the end of the day" and "As it relates to" also infiltrated her schtick as if to compensate for a wholesale lack of substance. "Crystal clear" manifested no more clearly than mud. The "trooof" she projected was anything but. She bloviated disparagingly as someone far more intelligent than other people, the King's English be damned. The bodacious butcheries of the language did nothing to flatter the Supermayor habitually 30 minutes late for meetings as groveling commoners and colleagues anticipated her arrival.

DeAndre Rucker, owner of Rucker Holdings, unraveled a contentious political ploy that prevented his cigar lounge from opening: "We were treated in Dolton unfairly. We received our permits and now (Mayor Tiffany Henyard) is revoking our permits because we won't fire one of our employees (the company's CFO, Kiana Belcher)."

IamJ9eve praises Trustee Belcher for her intuition:

"Nothin' slips past the Belcher. She is a pristine listener. She catches every bit of bullshit, like inflection and all—everything."

"She'll have the police follow you and give tickets," Belcher said. "I went out of town and one of the officers gave me tickets. It is a manipulation tactic."

The princess of pettiness pancaked any obstruction in her path. According to the president of the separate park district, Cleo Jones, some of his workers were fined $500 apiece for spreading mulch on playgrounds without a permit. Henyard was furious that Jones had allowed trustees to hold a meeting in one of the district's buildings because they were locked out of the chambers in Dolton.

"What do you mean we can't come in?" resident Cheryl Hall wondered. "Why can't people come in? This is a government building."

With Village Hall closed, trustees literally met outside as a meager assortment of residents descended. In a ridiculous scenario, an elderly female attendee admonished one of Henyard's original toadies, Donkor Parker, for rudely skulking behind her while sniping at the trustees. Henyard rewarded Parker, the young man hugging her blissfully the night she was appointed, by firing him from his job at the township.

Another meeting was moved from the village chambers to a small room in the basement. It lasted four minutes, preventing the participation of the media and residents, who by law must be afforded the chance to comment publicly.

"I was told by a security guard that I was not allowed upstairs where the boardroom meeting is," Josh Bootsma of the Lansing Journal said.

At one point, parking at Village Hall was cordoned off. "You made the elderly and disabled walk here," complained Thelma Price, who was wearing a black top with "YA'LL GOING TO JAIL" in white letters. "I hope you're proud of yourself, Tiffany Henyard. You're not going to understand until they come and put cuffs on you."

AK COLE asked the east Chicago native and daughter of politically engaged parents, how Henyard reacted to the blaring message: "If you watch her, she doesn't care. I care about what the world is thinking, not her. She put us on the map for the wrong reasons," Price said.

The organizers of an annual car show discovered barricades blocking the entrance to the park. They learned Henyard was worried the show would compete with one of her events.

The owner of Wood's Kitchen in Dolton felt her wrath: "I've heard rumors that say 'hey' I'm on the wrong team. I think I've been targeted because of my association, affiliation with a certain group of people—the trustees I've cooked for, the trustees."

"Momma" IamJ9eve is a proud mother whose verbal acumen outshines Henyard's. Through big glasses, she follows taped and live meetings with incessantly talkative analysis, laughter, light-hearted humming and crooning, and the ability to titillate her audience. Her mission statement, however, is concise: "Humor is medicine for the emotionally wounded. Laugh it off!"

"Bam, boom, got it nailed," says the long-haired host ramping up the computer for another eagerly anticipated LIVE rendition of the greatest show on Earth thanks to streaming by Reality Check TV. "Judy. Rich. Jimmy. David." She greets some of her listeners individually as they jump on board the cyber train, urging them to "Please make sure you hit the Like button for Momma, please, please, please, and thank you."

Moderators are important to her program. She calls them "dependables" affectionately. "We only time out people once it's confirmed they are trolls." Momma says that a second confirmation is typically reason enough to block them from intruding. She enlists moderator Matt: "You been around Momma for a long ass time, honey."

She later adds: "Momma like it when someone give Tiff the business."

In this meeting, Tiff-Tiff as described by Momma, inflames emotions after making one of her tired blanket statements: "My spirit in the right place. And people try to take that from me."

IamJ9eve adherents:

"If you ain't lyin', whatcha gonna do?"

"Look at her face—she believe what she sayin' or no?"

Henyard: "I'm everywhere and they (her detractors) never there."

IamJ9eve: "If they push her out, she gonna be a rapper."

The disaster known as Soooooopermayor, akin to a horrific accident or a bad B movie, sparks genuine, vicarious, and ghoulish intrigue as IamJ9eve urges her followers to be steadfast:

"Make sure you subscribe. Keeps Momma here and not there. You tube can be finicky. Dr. Marilyn in the house."

Henyard pitched fits at trustees in both jurisdictions:

"They lie up here so much, it don't make no sense. Every night I got to prove my love. They lie 'cause they can't beat me."

The publisher of the Lansing Journal newspaper was interviewed extensively by You tuber AK COLE, another deputy forming the Podcaster Posse tracking the Henyard hysteria.

"Sometimes in this modern day of interwebs, informing the community means informing the nation or even informing the world and that is what is going on with the Tiffany Henyard saga. People all over the world are interested in it following the videos we post and the videos many other people are posting," said Melanie Jongsma of the Journal, located in one of the township villages. "So, that is how I got to know somebody named AK COLE who is a You tuber and has also been following Thornton Township and Dolton and Tiffany Henyard. And so, he asked if he could interview me because I am local to the drama."

Jongsma alluded to the unpleasant buzz and frustration engulfing the community.

"We get comments on our videos from Australia and Germany. And it's been a ride. And the general consensus is that nobody can believe this is happening. She is so brazen. The people (of the township) have been active. The people have been reaching out to higher levels of government for help with this and the government has been silent."

Democratic Governor J.R. Pritzker, when queried about the Henyard debacle, basically said the state was deferring to the federal government and a probe by former Chicago Mayor Lori Lightfoot that village trustees bankrolled, a stance that many people considered betrayal. Pritzker wistfully toured the White House in the twilight of Joe Biden's presidency.

"We are small fish. They won't come for her because she is a single woman and a black woman," a resident said.

Pritzker, a multi-billionaire and investor, spent millions of his fortune supporting the Democratic party and battling for the state's highest office. The richest politician in the United States and a descendent of the Hyatt corporation family, Pritzker rode the crest of labor unions on the campaign trail. He advances liberal policies pertaining to immigration, cannabis, and gun control, among others.

"The thing people immediately assume is that for some reason the higher-ups are protecting Tiffany Henyard," the publisher posited, noting the hybrid mayor/supervisor probably lacked requisite shrewdness for widespread subterfuge. "She doesn't seem that politically connected."

AK COLE is a pleasant New Yorker donning a Yankees ball cap who furnishes no mission statement at his site other than "Your support is greatly appreciated!" He asked Jongsma about an FBI probe that kicked off in early 2024 with no obvious results.

"My understanding is that she is under investigation at Dolton and at Thornton Township by the FBI," she said. Agents subpoenaed records concerning payroll, employment matters, expenses, financials, and alleged co-mingling of funds between the two governments entities.

"That's like the number one question I get," interjected AK COLE in his placid, albeit cavernous voice. "How long do these investigations take? I think people are waiting on You tube and Facebook for the moment the FBI comes in, arrests her. Is it gonna be this big perp walk and stuff?"

Jongsma responded: "We want it to be dramatic, don't we? Wouldn't it be great if it were during a meeting when everybody was there? It's hard to be patient. I don't know what other evidence they need, but in the meantime people are suffering."

AK COLE was curious about public opinion of Henyard.

"Even if you don't have evidence of credit card charges and budget deficits, I think most people see through her. That's clear on You tube. The comment we get on You tube, and consensus is 'how can she be in office?'" Jongsma said. "The way she treats people in meetings, you wouldn't want to vote for somebody like that. Her supporters tend to be the people who have won something at bingo or have received free services from her. She encourages them to speak up (at meetings). She shouts down the people who are speaking out against her. There's a lot of yelling. There's a lot of chaos."

She mentioned frequent claims made by Henyard that the budgets are robust while refusing to produce formal documentation and ignoring FOIA (Freedom of Information Act) requests.

AK COLE: "How do you think she got all this attention on You tube and on TikTok and on Facebook? How did this local mayor get this much attention this quick?"

Jongsma: "I want to shout-out all the You tubers that have been helpful in this case. The public at Thornton Township meetings is trying to leverage social media. A lot of people have their phones up and they're recording it, they're sharing it to their Facebook channels, and their You tube channels. We were there from the beginning. You tube showed up next and really blew it up. This has been a convergence of local media, Chicago broadcast media, and You tube."

Ben Bradley and Regina Waldroup, of WGN and NBC Chicago respectively, trailed the Supermayor for the duration.

Henyard developed an obsession with blasting the media, AK COLE observed. "She always claims you guys are never in the township to cover the good news, it's always the bad news to make her look bad."

"That is not true," Jongsma replied. "We are at the meetings because that is where the business of the township is conducted." The Henyard administration has been obstructionist, she said, deliberately exempting a Journal reporter from covering a Black History Month celebration.

Supervisor Zuccarelli, according to the publisher, was known for putting on special events, something that placed Henyard under a microscope for doing. The difference, she told AK COLE, is that they are only appropriate once official business is thoroughly vetted. "The township is not just a party center. She likes being the center of attention. She likes (championing herself and the events) on Facebook."

Further, she said trustees may have been caught off guard by Zuccarelli's passing—they were accustomed to his knowledge of Robert's Rules of Order, experience presiding over meetings, and organizational skills.

Zuccarelli crafted a storied political career in Thornton Township, serving as supervisor for almost 30 years. His longevity accumulated a annual salary of well over $200,000, more than the governor. Calling his "Z" team "advocates for the people," the township containing some of the poorest communities in Illinois was millions of dollars in the black when he died. An Air Force medic in Vietnam, he also helmed the South Suburban College board of trustees for many years. Zuccarelli affiliated with Habitat for Humanity, the township youth committee, substance abuse prevention initiatives, and a disabled veterans' group. Tax rebates for residents, free transportation and 13 meal locations with blood pressure testing for the elderly were among his accomplishments. He endorsed Barack Obama's U.S. Senate run in 2004. Zuccarelli's well-oiled Democratic political machine was accused of too much patronage, paying $61,000 to a business owner tied to his committees, spending $106,000 to ballyhoo a Nobel peace prize for a South Carolina African American church that suffered a mass shooting, and traveling there with a group of 14 people at a cost of $46,000.

AK COLE's interview with the newspaper publisher rendered any malfeasance by Zuccarelli epically entrenched but comparatively modest while accounting for the irresistible Tiffany Henyard excitement hypnotizing the nation.

Early in her tenure at the township, former Trustee Jim Giglio accused Henyard of spending funds carelessly and preferring Dolton over the other villages.

"Watch what you say, I will get you for defamation of character," Henyard said.

"You're an elected official—I can say anything I want to. Sue me! Sue me!" Giglio shouted. "You promising to follow in Frank Zuccarelli's footsteps, and you're spitting on his grave."

The Lansing Journal, carrying the motto "Inform and Connect," was especially watchful for offensive posts at its You tube site during the Henyard years, mandating thoughtfulness and respect, no foul language or personal attacks, and rarely accepting anonymous messages, a deviation from the wild, wild West of podcasting.

Following the story "Fact Check: Thornton Township did not face deficit in 2022, as Henyard claims," Jongsma and Managing Editor Carole Sharwarko only allowed the comment "She is a liar" after serious debate about whether it was inordinately abusive. In truth, citizens have traditionally been protected more from opinionated assaults than public officials in mainstream media.

"I know it (the Henyard story) is important but I kind of hate devoting that much attention to this circus because there is so much other good news in our community that deserves reporting," Jongsma said.

Unfortunately, as they say, the show must go on. And it did.

Former Chicago mayor and federal prosecutor Lori Lightfoot unveiled her findings at a regular Village of Dolton board meeting as residents gasped, hooted, and hollered, saying she experienced their dismay as the fiscal disaster was being excavated. "I know how I felt when I started seeing some of these numbers, so I can imagine how all of you are feeling after all of this time in the dark."

In two years, spanning April 2022 to May of 2024, the village coffers dropped from a $5.6 million surplus to $3.6 million in arrears, fueled by mismanagement, a paucity of documentation and the careless use of six credit cards rarely showing receipts for purchases that spiked to $780,000 in 2023. She cited the Henyard fiefdom's lack of transparency about payroll records and vendor transactions as her microphone "inexplicably" malfunctioned. She also suspected the Henyard goons of pilfering a tangible portion of $3 million allocated by the American Rescue Plan to the Village of Dolton.

There were no technical difficulties plaguing the presiding Supermayor's patented gold mouthpiece when she subjected Lightfoot to a tirade: "How dare you come into somebody's town and start working or doing something even though we said something saying it's illegal. You were once a mayor too. You should not be disrespectful like that."

"Beginning at least as early as late 2021, there was concerted, systematic effort on behalf of Mayor Henyard and others in her administration to hide the true financial condition of the Village of Dolton from the trustees and from members of the public," Lightfoot said. "There are many allegations that we received that Mayor Henyard ordered village personnel to simply stop responding to FOIA's (Freedom of Information Act requests). We were not able to verify the allegations, in part because village employees who reported directly to Mayor Henyard did not cooperate in the investigation."

Thelma Price credited Lightfoot for a "fabulous job," vindicating the trustees in fiscal lay terms residents could understand.

A prolific member of the Tiffany Henyard Podcaster Posse and one of the earliest to track the decadence, Hannibal Is Hungry offers relaxed cadence, in-depth explanations and careful research from his digs in New York.

The FBI inquiry into purported fudging of funds and other misdeeds bridged podcasters and elected officials disgusted with the Supermayor.

"We shouldn't have to ask as trustees, beg people (Henyard and her government minions) for what we want but they want our votes (to approve the mayor's agenda)," said Village of Dolton Trustee Kiana Belcher, who also called the Supermayor a "self" servant rather than a "public" one.

Trustee Brittney Norwood chimed in: "We need this money. We have to operate as a village. And if they continue to spend money we don't have, it has to come from somewhere. We have credit card spending that is unaccounted for."

Henyard exploded on Instagram: "Trustees been stealing the taxpayers money. Here's proof!! Ask yourself why didn't Lori Lightfoot report this? Why is everyone involved in the cover up involving the trustees? The writing is on the wall…Residents don't let them continue stealing from you."

"Are we going to finally see the downfall of Supermayor Tiffany Henyard?" Hannibal Is Hungry asks. "The mayor has locked them (trustees) out of important software that is supposed to show transparency."

In rambling Facebook fury, Henyard threatened to have her political opponents arrested. "I will be pressing charges. And that's just me telling you a little bit because all the pointing the finger at Tiffany—lyin' on me —I'm over it."

Hannibal Is Hungry removes his glasses and takes off the gloves: "Henyard only hires people she knows, cronies at exorbitant salaries, even if they are not qualified," comparing the mayor to a "kingpin" perpetrating "mafia-type stuff" by "using the taxpayers' dollars like her own personal piggy bank."

The allegations stimulate a barrage of threads from the internet stratosphere:

"hundreds of thousands of people can see she's stealing, she's crazy, people are taking time to pin rap lyrics to (her) crimes."

"Her mugshot isn't hard to find."

"Nate The Lawyer made a video on this and brought up a search results showing this Mayor was actually arrested in 2016 for Criminal Trespass of Vehicles and had to pay $1,500 bond. So, she has a criminal record and is still breaking the law. How they didn't see this when doing a background check, if they even did one, is beyond me."

"I work in a prosecutor's office and I showed this story to one of my lawyer friends and her jaw hit the floor. I can't believe this kind of thing can happen, it's nuts."

"If she doesn't go to prison for fraud than I know this country is screwed!"

"What a disgrace."

"Hearing her speak one sentence should be enough to know she was unqualified. You get what you voted for."

"She HAS A CRIMINAL RECORD at the time she was elected. She was NOT properly vetted. She's now dipping her fingers in the biggest pot of CASH she's EVER seen."

"This is one of the worst cases of public chiropraction. I've ever seen and I'm in Detroit."

"I have all the respect in the world for the employees and trustees that have been relentless on their transparency and being vocal on the issues."

"Just imagine all she had to do…is do the right thing. She was blessed to get those 2 positions (mayor and supervisor) and could have led a comfortable life, but instead she got greedy and let it go to her head."

"Excellent reporting. Thank you."

"Most informative video I have seen so far, good work!"

Hannibal Is Hungry garnered the adulation of Jongsma at the Lansing Journal:

"Named after the North African general who crossed the Alps on elephants to defend against the Roman invasion, it is perhaps not surprising that Hannibal Darby is also in the business of defending against the powerful. Darby was active on You tube long before Henyard's outrageous behavior made her a viral sensation. A gig worker trying to provide for his family, he named his channel Hannibal Is Hungry to affirm how seriously he takes his work. The name also evokes Hannibal Lecter, the cannibalistic serial killer in the 1991 movie Silence of the Lambs, and Darby thought the play on words might help him stand out online."

From his first Henyard video, Thornton Township residents commenced emailing him. "They were so desperate for help," Hannibal said. "They tried to reach out to their attorney general and the governor, and all these people, and they were not getting enough attention to it. I think they were feeling that no one seems to care."

The sympathy in cyberspace for Henyard's victims was not lost on Paul Robertz, an ardent meeting attendee and crusader for the township and municipality who happens to be a white man wedded to Jennifer, a black woman, in the heavily African American community.

"We've made a lot of new friends. Her outrageous behavior has spawned a whole people's movement," Robertz said while lauding a "new crop of journalists" providing commentary on social media.

The middle-aged, bespectacled Robertz finished only part of a prepared statement before two of Henyard's goons, Michael Smith and dreadlocked Demarkus Criggley, enveloped him at the podium. The mayor's married live-in boyfriend, Kamal "Cigarette Break" Woods, making six figures running the village's murky youth violence prevention program, and Keith Price were also part of the Henyard contingent. Robertz had reminded residents, trustees, and Henyard that humans, when behaving like animals, warrant a swift whack on the snout. A handful of screaming female audience members stood up for Robertz as he retreated. Indeed, coercion and disruptions prevailed in public meetings during the Supermayor's tenure.

Robertz was figuratively down, but not out. His comprehensive, exacting letter to the editor of the Lansing Journal enveloped the rising angst of people in the township tired of complicit crickets in the Democrat party, of which he was a member, at the state capital.

Dear Governor Pritzker or Anne Caprera, Chief of Staff:

"I reside in Lansing, IL, within Thornton Township. For the last year, I have spent a good portion of my time watching Tiffany Henyard, the township's unqualified supervisor and mayor of Dolton, IL. I will assume you are aware of many of her crimes:

Misappropriation of funds

Obstruction of justice regarding murders by her police force

Co-mingling of funds between Dolton and Thornton Township

Locking residents and trustees out of village hall

Denying the press and the public entry to township board meetings

Using public funds for campaign materials

Hiding financial records and proposed budgets, etc.

I will assume that you are aware the Village of Dolton no longer makes payments for their employees' health insurance or pension funds, so now the Supermayor looks toward the township to fund an increasing number of parties in an attempt to distract the gullible. She prevents trustees in Dolton and in Thornton Township from placing any items on board meeting agendas. I will be happy to clarify any questions you may have about crimes she is alleged to have committed. However, that is not the purpose of this letter.

I am one of the residents who is tired of making public comments at board meetings which never lead to any action by the Henyard administration. We are tired of hearing of Tiffany's anger at those critical of her, and toward the news media who report accurately. She calls it 'fake news,' telling residents to do our research to get the whole story. However, her lack of transparency and orders to block FOIA (Freedom of Information Act) requests prevent us from doing our research. When she promises to show us 'da troof,' she merely insults her critics or has one of her henchmen tell us that her predecessor was just as bad. What bothers me most is the way she doubles down, insisting that she is Dr. King's dream, and was chosen by God to hold two positions of leadership, while she continues on her course without even one apology.

The purpose of this email is to convey to you the great disappointment residents have in our Governor and in Attorney General Raoul. Governor Pritzker, we are well aware that you do not wish to interfere with the FBI or Lightfoot investigations. However, those investigations are for federal crimes. Our disappointment and frustration is that Tiffany Henyard is able to stay in power so long, unfettered by any state law enforcement. We are unable to get the Illinois State Police or Cook County Sheriff to police the Dolton Police when they prohibit citizens from attending public meetings.

It is not the job of the FBI to enforce the Illinois Open Meetings Act. Lori Lightfoot cannot force the Henyard administration to answer FOIA requests. The attorney general has made many rulings that the Henyard administration has violated. The IL OMA (Office of Monetary Affairs), and has demanded (in vain) that Thornton Township provide the information a resident requests under FOIA. In every case I am aware of, the attorney general has never taken any concrete action to penalize the Village of Dolton, Thornton Township, Tiffany Henyard, or members of her administration. Therefore she has no incentive to obey state law if doing so does not please her. When federal agents delivered the first subpoenas to Dolton Village Hall in April (of 24), Tiffany Henyard, her married boyfriend, and the acting deputy police chief of the Dolton Police Department immediately drove to Springfield for counsel.

Yes, it appears that Tiffany Henyard is enjoying protection from the Democratic Party of Illinois. She brags that she was elected with 82% of the vote—which was her winning percentage in Dolton's 2021 general election. The Democratic primary was a very close race between Tiffany, the former mayor (Riley Rogers) who had just suffered a stroke, and a non-Dolton resident who is now charged with sexual assault on a tax-funded trip to Las Vegas.

There are very few Republicans here, although in recent months I have heard many former Democrats state that they will vote for a Republican or independent candidate in the next election. The reality is that voter turnout for local elections throughout Thorntown Township is between 10% and 15% of registered voters. This means that Tiffany's campaign does not have to buy many votes with gas giveaways, parties, boxes of food, new TVs, and appliances as bingo prizes.

I note that Thornton Township pays $10,000 per month in political consulting fees to Cornerstone Government Affairs and another $5,000 in lobbying fees to the former state senator who is the mentor of the chair of the Senate Appropriations Committee. Henyard insists on hiring well-connected attorney Michael DelGado to represent the Village of Dolton, Thornton Township, and even the school boards in Thornton Township. The indicted Village Administrator (Keith Freeman) is close to House Speaker Chris Welch.

Many of us feel that when these powerful members of the Democratic Party of Illinois initially supported Tiffany Henyard, they had no idea how brazen her corruption would become. Governor Pritzker, is the reason for a lack of state investigation into Tiffany Henyard the fear that such an investigation may lead to incriminating evidence against politicians holding higher positions than hers?

I speak for many other residents of Thornton Township, including quite a few who also live in Dolton, when I ask: 'Has Tiffany Henyard become an embarrassment to Governor Pritzker or those high up in the Democratic Party of Illinois? If you have paid any attention to the worldwide press covering her, you noticed that the most common from those learning about her for the first time is: 'How in the world is she still in office?'

Having worked and lived amongst them, I cannot blame the voters of Dolton for the longevity of her political career. Doltonites are not dolts. They voted to recall her, not knowing that Tiffany would bill taxpayers for her legal fees from the well-connected attorneys who helped her get her recall overturned.

It seems that she has now stolen enough of our tax dollars to buy her way into the elite part of our justice system that gives immunities from prosecution to our wealthiest politicians. She seems to flaunt her elevated status, constantly telling the helpless residents, 'I love you, and there's nothing you can do about it.'

We will appreciate your answer to the most common question: 'Why is Tiffany Henyard still in office?' We would also appreciate help with some level of county or state law enforcement against the criminal organization that controls the governments in Dolton and Thornton Township. But, to be honest, we do not expect more than talk from the governor's office.

It would be great to have our expectations exceeded, but it is more important that you provide an answer to our question within the next seven days, before the Democratic National Convention comes to our area. I have contacts at the Lansing Journal, WGN 9 TV, and NBC 5 who will publish your response or lack thereof."

Sincerely,

Paul Robertz, Disappointed Democrat

Save a docile drip, drip from Springfield, and any maneuvering behind the scenes, Governor Pritzker and his bureaucrats were derisively unruffled.

One of the ladies confronting the toughs threatening Robertz was 45-year-old Vivian Allen, mostly confined to a walker because of a brain tumor that should have killed her. "Every time I go to a meeting, I just get enraged because I just think about the lies that she told," said Allen, swearing to pursue Henyard until she is booted off her high horse. Hope soared that "she was the person to come in and help Dolton, and we believed it."

Vindictive Keith Price messaged Allen:

"You're sick because of your bitterness and wickedness…your cancer will come back ten times harder if you keep up such behavior… you have been warned!"

A Hannibal Is Hungry listener lacerates him:

"if Price wrote that it's abhorrent, disgusting, and there aren't enough adjectives to describe just how terrible it is…meaning he probably wrote it. if an actual politician at a higher level said that, that could easily cost them their career."

"We have seen him time and time again bully residents of both TT and Dolton at meetings," Anna Menchaca wrote on Facebook. "In the real world and in a real professional setting where background checks are performed Keith Price would never have secured employment, much less be given an administrative position with subordinates he could abuse."

Resident Darius Pendleton was not afraid of Price: "I've been waiting to bump back into KP. It's obvious he knows who to and who not to play with. He is no tough Tony at all. Hooters was our last encounter as he had the hen with him. To act as if you're going to do something to me…..or even record my car when he could have approached me as a man inside…..closure is needed…..and I've never gotten closure."

Replies:

"Darius Pendleton, go to the TT meeting Tues night, he will probably be there, we need more men to attend the meetings."

"Darius Pendleton you can tell he pick and choose. The coward can barely walk, he picks women or frail men to intimidate or assault."

Price often inexplicably sat in the front row, directly across from Henyard and the trustees. One night, without having been granted the floor to speak, he interrupted Chris Gonzalez, precipitating a heated exchange.

"What about us? What about us? What about our fears? What about our tax dollars?" yelled Vivian Allen at the mayor who, as usual, looked down dismissively. Allen's anger over money harkened memories of 2022 when Trustee Ed Steave urged the mayor against hastily approving budgets:

"(For the last eight years) we went through every budget line by line, which takes hours. We cannot pass this without it being public. We're not saying we're against the budget—we're just saying be transparent with it."

"Ed Steave just asked me to do his work," Henyard grumbled. "We're not gonna discuss the budget. There's no need to waste any more of the people's time. We may as well go ahead, pass it along, and go to the next agenda item. I'm asking the board of trustees to humble themselves, to have some love in y'all's hearts for these residents and give them what's owed to them, what's due to them."

She reminded everyone in the meeting of the unprecedented street repairs and maintenance, housing upgrades, and tree-trimming services provided to residents by her administration.

At her highness's behest, the Village of Dolton paid O.A.K.K. Construction Company, a defendant in multiple corruption cases, $205,000 in zero bids and no-contract work to replace senior homeowners' roofs and windows.

The board had not authorized the projects and initially refused to pay. When the company threatened homeowners with liens, though, the village covered the bill with federal COVID-19 funds.

"I am really confused right now," resident Rose Rice said. "First of all, I didn't sign any papers or an agreement with this company, so why is this lien against my property and why is my name on this document? This is asinine."

Trustee Steave detailed the conundrum: "If you don't get a bid, you get contractors who donate to her campaign fund. That's reality. Because the mayor should not have all the power to pick contractors, pick who she wants, and then she goes to them for campaign donations."

Henyard said the conventional bidding process was unnecessary: "I don't go pick people. People come to the village, they apply, and they want to do it, and they do the work. I could care less who does it as long as the resident gets the service."

Cooking With Frank introduces the "Dolton Chainsaw Massacre" episode highlighting her obsession with trees, accompanied by video of men toiling in earnest and Henyard squawking and pawing through free boxes of food being distributed following a storm that knocked out electricity.

"She's back on the tree-cuttin' so that lets me know some money is bein' exchanged where it shouldn't be. Or, on the other hand, she done pieced together a little clique of niggers and they rented a couple of pieces of equipment from Home Depot, and she promised them $30 or $40, or somethin' like that. No legitimate contractor would do this type of work under Tiffany anymore. She already owes one of them companies like 400 racks."

Levity from listeners ensues:

"I'm glad AG Tactical sent me your way. You have the wit and personality to make a terrible situation humorous. God bless the citizens of Dolton."

"They are fly by night's because there's no hard hats no high visibility vests it's totally again OSHA regulations"

"Why is the city responsible to cut down trees inside peoples property lines? Also she mows people grass? wtf that is an owner's responsibility"

"What happens if a worker is injured from a heavy tree while cleaning up. What's the bet non of those workers are covered by insurance of henyard's cleanup crew?"

"Did the Supermayor use the leaves from the trees for her hair do?"

"She need to clean dat wig it crazy!!!"

"Dem eyebrows spray painted on"

"Did she just refer to apples as vegetables?

"That's a food bank box, $3"

"Shit, no chitlins?"

"Thighs and gizzards liver bowel and toenails as well as chicken feet"

Dan Lee moved to Dolton 35 years ago from Chicago where he grew up in the projects. The suburb portended safety and prosperity. Despite a drive-by shooting that endangered him at home, Lee appreciates the community and was a fixture at meetings, one of which constable Lewis Lacey kicked him out of. "I don't like bullies," said the crisply cogent, deep-voiced public speaker.

"They (her goons) have nothing else to do. They're going to leave with her. We can just cleanse the whole township of these reprobates, of these people that try to intimidate. Those people gravitate to each other. We got to get our village and township back," Lee said.

He also invented one of the most hysterical one-liners pegging the Supermayor: "This woman would not understand respect if Aretha Franklin came back from the grave. She has no concept of respect."

When Henyard barked "Your time is up" at Lee, he said: "Your time is up too."

Probably in his 60s, the physically fit Lee not only contradicts his years but resented Henyard's penchant for race rattling. "All that person has to say is I'm black, you can't talk to me about that. That makes no sense to me. People who fall for that are not paying attention to what is going on around them."

Lee's feelings were echoed emphatically at another regular meeting by a black lady. "It (the criticism) has nothing to do with shaming a black woman in power nor shaming the Supermayor as you so infinitely call yourself."

Vivian Allen assailed the Supermayor's racial myopia:

"As a black woman, we are all ashamed and embarrassed of Tiffany Henyard. She does not speak for the African American community in Dolton. She speaks for her and her goons. It's people of color that don't like her. Race has nothing to do with it."

It was not long before public comments, once inviting dialogue with trustees and the mayor at the end of meetings, were moved to the beginning with no Q and A permitted. Henyard advised citizens to call or email department heads with inquiries that were rarely acknowledged. Genuine discourse with her brood dissipated, and she brutalized the gallery with rambling dissertations aggrandizing herself and detouring concerns.

Public safety also waned, along with retirement provisions, health care benefits, and insurance. "(Union) members are getting their claims denied," Dolton firefighter Adam Farej said. "When the mayor first started to run, we did endorse her, then everything went sideways."

Just Doing Nails listeners aren't having it:

"Stealing the firefighters pension is beyond evil."

"There're things you need in a big/small city. Firefighters being one. What would people do without them?"

"Stealing the firemen's pension now that's playing with fire...when you call them for an emergency I'm sure they will be delayed."

Kiana Belcher pushed back decisively when Henyard hand-picked five individuals for the police and fire commission with virtually no vetting or review of credentials by the trustees: Phillip Williams, Robert Sherrill, William Fletcher, Brenda Richardson and, unsurprisingly, Stanley Brown, whom she initially referred to as Stanley Moore.

"They (trustees) the puppets," Henyard said. "I'm not joining that circus."

Counters Just Doing Nails: "I feel like she has a good enough circus going right now."

Cyber critiques:

"I think she wanted people in those positions so she could 'instruct' them on how to do the job...giving Tiffany the power to oversee these departments as well! She wanted to set those positions up with more 'yes people.'"

"Tiff, put it in writing with resumes. This is a Public Safety issue. Put the Citizens first."

Farej added that firefighters hesitated to speak out for fear of reprisal.

There may have been reprisal when nine bullets riddled a white sedan parked outside the home of former Dolton Trustee Valeria Stubbs, a fierce critic of Henyard and recall organizer, according to the Chawanne Burns podcast. Security camera footage recorded two men running from an alley and driving away at a high rate of speed in a small SUV.

"They refused to give me the police report (about the shooting) and I haven't heard anything since. We don't trust the police here," said Stubbs, who claimed a "caravan" of cops and city workers tried to terrorize her at home.

A viewer hopes that the host of Mob Vlog doesn't meet a worse fate:

"What up guys...I keep lookin' over Adam's shoulder waitin' for a hit man to break through for Tiffany Henyard."

"What happened to all the black love? Where is it at? Black power, and we need to stick with each other? I guess that's out the door if you don't agree with (Henyard)," Burns says.

"Follow the money to my bank account. She don't give a crap about black, she only cares about green," a Mob Vlog follower posts.

Documentarian Tommy G visited Dolton with his crew after witnessing Tik Tok videos of Henyard.

He was on a junket to find out whether local sentiment deemed her a hero or a villain. "She's a villain. She really don't be doin' nothin' for us," a young White Castle hamburger worker asserted. "She try to make a big show, a big act, but she's not doin' the stuff that really needs to be done."

Recognizing Henyard's arrogance, Valeria Stubbs told Tommy G: "I really don't think she thinks she is going to jail."

Upon arriving at Village Hall, Tommy G was met by Henyard flunkey William Moore who said they needed permission to cover the story despite being on public property. After Deputy Chief Lacey forced them to leave the foyer of the building, Tommy G and his cameramen were surrounded by half-a-dozen police officers in the parking lot and required to produce identification.

A recent village employee called Lacey "one of the mayor's lynchmen."

Stephanie Wiedeman recounted that she was ticketed by Dolton police for removing Henyard's campaign flyer from the windshield of her car.

"Tiffany, Officer Lacey, and their cronies are not only bullies of the worst kind but an actual disgrace to the title of public servant," said Tommy G, who later challenged the deputy chief to a skirmish in a martial arts gym that was not reciprocated. "The goons have come out."

"Smash them Likes."

"Hit that Subscribe."

"It's that time again."

"Cooking With Frank."

This episode features colorful AI graphics and technology welcoming viewers to the holiday season with fireplace ambiance in a family room, ice skating at a large mall, serenity outside a decorated craftsman house, a happy couple dressed for the season, and two men relaxing over cups of hot chocolate.

A holiday hiatus, of sorts, from the Henyard heresy.

He wishes Merry Christmas to his listeners and subscribers while eschewing the same for the Supermayor and her minions. As a closeup of Henyard talking incessantly defiles the screen, Frank asks "Would it be petty of me to have some people that I wish to have a fucked-up Christmas? This is one of my favorites, you know, that I hope has a terrible ass Christmas, and that's Hair Hat Tubman. This could be the last Christmas that she spends as a free woman, for a good little minute."

Other suspects in crime endure deviation from the holiday spirit, beginning with the balding, "raggedy" Trustee Andrew Holmes dancing at the block party that feted Henyard's Village of Dolton election toward the beginning of this book. Holmes's hairline, Frank says, is a like a baseball game: "Way back, way back, and it's gone!"

He says "Keithopotamus" Price is in it for the money bestowed by her highness. Kamal "Cigarette Break" Woods, according to Frank, revs the engine that swells her mammoth ego. And Cooking With Frank detests Trustee Stanley Brown for straddling the political fence:

"You can't make a fuckin' decision to save your life. One minute we think you with us and the next minute you at Tiffany Henyard's (gathering) with about 15 other people. You sittin' over there in the corner like nobody see your ass. The lights was on, Stanley. We saw you."

Sheriff Frank's fans light up the exchange like a Christmas tree:

"Frank, your artwork at the beginning is absolutely beautiful."

"Happy New Year Frank. Keep it coming!"

"Merry Christmas brother"

"Keith SIMPapotamus is pitiful…Lying for Thieffany. Carmen CARLISLE gets my thumbs up."

"4am Boxing Day in North Wales and delighted to see this stream pop up—liked before I watched and with a marvelous introduction—thank you Frank—Merry Christmas"

"Man I love all your content! At this point I smash the Like before I even watch your video. Thank you for your coverage of the Tiffany Henyard story."

"Never laughed so much, don't think Tiffany will have a good Christmas with what she's facing."

"Keep up the good work, and nicknames educating people in a humorous way. They need it from every angle!! Little do some residents know those Bingo prizes aren't free because they paid for them with their Sales tax."

Perhaps a grinch to the Supermayor's sycophants, the Podcaster Posse contributor reprimands residents, many of them elderly, for drinking Henyard's spiked eggnog as he prepares for Christmas: "They expect their grass cut. They want their electric bill paid--their rent paid. They wanna go play bingo and win all kinds of free shit," Frank says, worrying that they are "about to vote for Tiffany on some bullshit."

Henyard sensationalized "Big Bingo" every third Thursday of the month, procuring complimentary air dryers, televisions, refrigerators, stoves, and washers and dryers as prizes.

There were cyber cynics:

"Show us the Receipts"

"Thornton Township now purchases appliances to furnish homes of Henyard supporters who win Big Bingo prizes"

"Tiffany just give out Lowes and home depot credit cards. I can get what I want. Thank you in advance! I don't have a good credit score so I need to play bingo to get a frig and stove. By the way you can use the Township trucks for free delivery"

Incredibly, signs brandishing "Mayor Clark is worse than Tiffany Henyard" were hoisted at protests in the Thornton Township city of Harvey. A federal lawsuit levied accusations of extortion, corruption, and civil rights violations against Mayor Chris Clark, the police chief and deputy chief, and the administrator. A coalition of small businesses, community leaders, and activists instigated the suit citing suppression of free speech and police intimidation. City officials allegedly fleeced business owners under the guise of collecting unpaid property taxes with fines for tardiness ranging between $12,000 and $30,000, even placing concrete blockades around their establishments to ensure compliance. Clark allowed the Supermayor to hold a special meeting in Harvey, where the village purportedly violated state public records laws by withholding financial data, eerily reminiscent of the Henyard hijinks.

"There's so many corruption stories in Illinois. What is up with the water the politicians drink, especially in Cook County?" News For Reasonable People asks.

Foul water may also have been an issue in Tarrant, Alabama, where elected notoriety mirrored Henyard's. Mayor Wayman Newton, according to Hannibal Is Hungry, was accused of fiscal mismanagement, interfering with police investigations, and driving the town's sewer system into foreclosure.

Hannibal Is Hungry says the people are "trapped in the worst episode of 'The Office,'" as Newton idly tinkers on his cell phone during citizen comments.

Listeners blast the beleaguered mayors:

"Why it's always our people! The Blacks!!!!!!!!"

"Dolton, part 2. At least they have better microphones and video."

"Henyard 2.0. All of them appear to have a total I.Q. of around 50."

"Tiffany is the little girl mayor and this guy is the little boy mayor. His head down, on his phone like a little boy when someone is talking to him."

"He's probably texting Tiffany."

Nate The Lawyer compares Henyard to Mayor Khalid Khamou, known as Mayor Kobi, of South Fulton, Georgia, which has the highest percentage of blacks of any city in America with a population over 100,000.

"They have both been arrested. Remember Henyard was traveling all over the United States on the taxpayer dime? Instead of limiting it to the United States, he's traveling the world."

In three years, Khamou visited Paris twice, Colombia on three occasions, Africa two times, and Toronto at taxpayers' expense. Khamou, a burglary suspect, and active member of the Atlanta BLM (Black Lives Matter) chapter, was banned from municipal buildings, obliged to surrender his publicly financed city vehicle, a drone, pool table, and $20,000 personal studio.

Mayor Khamou borrowed Henyard's prideless playbook:

"Last night's 1AM vote was a coup by seven people to override the votes of thousands who chose me as mayor in 2021. Yet there's no way to defend my name without attacking other Black people which is exactly what those carving up South Fulton for trucking routes, warehouses and data centers are counting on. I am heartbroken to see us more willing to fight each other than our real enemies."

Nate's viewers stoke the coals:

"When u elect a person that has one platform…his own race…expect problems"

"How many cities run by woke, progressive mayors see improvements in their community, reduction in spending, reduction in crime, and well run practices?"

"Fulton, Dolton, wonder what's next."

A Just Doing Nails partisan remembers the more serene Dolton:

"OMG…50s 60s and 70s were wonderful in my village…there was no 10 mil in debt no murders no corruption no druggers and mugging and poverty. So what happened to my village? The south side of Chicago is only 5 minutes North of the village boundary."

The "Latina" Tiffany Henyard, Nate The Lawyers says, is Mayor Rachel Ruelas of Mabton, Washington where no budget has been presented in two years, its police officers resigned, and the only council member voting against a recall petition was her own mother. She gained business experience operating a bridal boutique. The frosting on the cake were restaurant fisticuffs between the mayor, her husband, their son, and another couple who both went to the emergency room.

"This sounds very familiar to Tiffany Henyard from Dolton, Illinois, who also ran her own burger shop before she transitioned to ruining that town as mayor," Nate adds.

Without a monopoly on infamy but earning a national reputation for pandemonium and leaving no stone unturned, the Supermayor created the Tiffany Henyard Cares Foundation in 2023, foisting "a mission to make a difference in the lives of breast cancer victims and their families. Through her unwavering commitment and the TH CARES Foundation, she brings hope, empowerment, and support to communities across the Township and the State of Illinois."

The township board negligently devoted $10,000 of taxpayers' money to the enterprise while government resources were used to solicit donations. The Supermayor spent another $17,000 on 1,000 white T-shirts and hoodies adorning a pink cancer ribbon circling CARES, a dubious attempt at generosity on the public dole. Administrator Keith Freeman filed the initial paperwork for the group and was one of its officers.

The Supermayor led a procession of bicyclists, pedestrians, and vans on a week-long venture to the state capital in Springfield to ballyhoo their cause. The legislature was not in session, no bill was filed on behalf of the organization, and $11,500 of public money was spent on motels, restaurants, and other amenities. The trip was featured in a video of the jubilant, prancing mayor energetically enthralling her toadies and presumably well-intentioned people who were swindled by the charade.

"What was the true intention here other than self-promotion?" Trustee Chris Gonzalez inquired.

Symbolically removing her wig, cancer survivor Vivian Allen boldly confronted Henyard at a meeting:

"You want to ignore me, right? All these victims out here—not victims, survivors—they all survivin' Henyard. This administration is shameful. Residents, I'm so sorry that she won't step down, especially 'cause survivors I love you, and ain't nothin' you can do about because I mean it. She doesn't mean it."

Henyard, accustomed to ducking scrutiny at the state level, watched as the attorney general's office pulled the plug on the nonprofit, saying Tiffany Henyard Cares could no longer solicit donations after missing multiple deadlines to produce legally required tax filings. According to a government spokesman, "The attorney general is committed to protecting donors from potential fraud and enforcing laws in place to ensure charitable organizations meet their financial responsibilities."

Henyard shirked responsibility for the initiative despite Trustee Carmen Carlisle's contrariness: "I worked as your assistant. I saw a lot; the first time I really ever questioned supporting you is when you went on this national platform, and you said you didn't know anything about the foundation. But you forget that I was in certain rooms when certain things happened."

Carlisle accused the Supermayor of "unethical and predatory behavior" afflicting many aspects of the community.

"I am seeking the removal of Carmen Carliar because she is a liar," Henyard squawked.

Carlisle: "Tiffany, the only person up here lyin' is you."

Carlisle's transformation from her days as a servile assistant was profound: "I'm just happy to be part of the administration. Also, mayor, people they come at you, they attack you, but I love that you keep pushin', keep pressin' no matter what. As long as you keep your eyes on God, he gonna always take care of you."

Henyard, Trustee Jerry Jones and Trustee Darlene Gray Everett voted down a proposal by Carlisle and Trustee Chris Gonzalez obligating vendors to receive board approval prior to performing services.

The only tag team in the Podcast Posse for the purposes of this book is Mob Vlog with Adam Flowers and Red Wemette, an FBI informant from 1971 to 1989 exposing organized crime in Chicago. Their podcast invitation is flavored accordingly:

"Step into the underbelly of American politics, Adam Flowers and Red Wemette, as we dive deep into the world of modern-day political machinations. Here on Mob Vlog, we explore the intricate web of influence, power, and sometimes, the less-than-savory dealings that define our nation's political landscape.

Adam Flowers, your intrepid guide, brings his sharp wit and incisive commentary to each episode, breaking down the complex into the digestible. Alongside him, Red Wemette, with his insider knowledge and street-smart perspective, adds depth and color to our discussions, making every detail of political life as gripping as a thriller."

Serious content, buoyed by a rapid montage of news flashes, is unable to overcome their propensities: "Welcome back guys, it's Adam Flowers. If you're tunin' in lookin' for news, this isn't the place, okay? We have fun with you guys."

Laughter lurches from Wenette, who says he is feeling "chipper" on the split screen.

Flowers: "We're just here to host the show and have fun talkin' about Tiffany. Please join in the comments. We do read 'em while we're talking."

Red laughs.

The tandem play movie clips to enhance their histrionics.

"We blow off steam and mix politics with, you know, a little Blazing Saddles," the goateed Flowers says as viewers levitate into the Mob Vlog cyber realm for information and entertainment. "Christina Morris. BSJ. Leanne Rolling. Scott Christoffel. Steve Martin—all the way from Scotland."

"She (Henyard) held a press conference. Did you see that? She aksed a lot of things," imitates Flowers.

Suddenly, demented Jack Nicholson chops threw a door with an axe in "The Shining," maniacally screaming "Heeeerrrrrreeee's Johnny!"

Flowers: "Here's what happens when you aks something."

Wemette: "She's always aksin' somethin'. That's what you call 'getting the axe.'"

"The shit show in Dolton is just unbelievable," Flowers says. "They don't have a police chief right now; there's no insurance for the township."

Red forecasts convictions and guilty pleas for Henyard, portending something roughly equivalent to what Tom Cruise said in a film about an adversary as the scene develops: "You're gonna get fucked with a dick big enough for an elephant to feel it."

An ongoing crawl of written comments perpetuates the interaction:

Missy Gilson: "Regina Waldroup of NBC did a great job with her report yesterday. It is an hour long. It's all about Tiffany and how she got started."

Duane Mansel: "Lightfoot investigation is a waste of money and worthless."

Wemette says Lightfoot's forays have merit because they should contribute to the federal case against the Supermayor, adding that Keith Freeman, besieged by bankruptcy fraud, is probably cutting a deal on his tax returns in exchange for assisting the FBI.

The Tiffany meal is delectable to the podcasters thanks to a recording of her mayoral inauguration:

"Aks not what you can do for your country, but aks what you can do for your country," bungles Henyard.

Robust laughter reverberates from the studio.

The silver screen furnishes another line with video from an old Western: "You use your tongue prettier than a $20 whore."

Viewer Sher Yelverton partakes in the unabashedly amusing attacks on the Supermayor:

"Tiff got an A and graduated with honors. Hooked on Ebonics. Dollar Tree. 1.25"

Mob Vlog co-host Red Wemette surely encountered the Chicago crime syndicate in concert with crooked mayors whose legacy is legendary. The city's early, enormous industrial growth fomented an era of unregulated capitalism ruled by WASP plutocrats such as Marshall Field and George Pullman anointing and controlling politicians for their own devices.

Once the Democratic party machine got rolling, working-class immigrant communities were often the beneficiaries. Chicago Mayor Anton Cermak, on the heels of the Depression, termed the party the "house for all peoples," currying Eastern European and African American voters converting from the Republican side of the equation.

According to the most powerful Chicago mayor of them all, Richard Daley, who mastered an astounding maze of connections in virtually every corner of the city's political and societal landscape:

"The party permits ordinary people to get ahead. Without the party, I couldn't be mayor. The rich guys can get elected on their money, but somebody like me, an ordinary person, needs the party. Without the party, only the rich would be elected to office."

Daley appeared on the cover of Mike Royko's book "Boss" dressed as an emperor, a male rendition of aspiring empress Supermayor Henyard on a much grander scale. His no-nonsense Chicago police subdued anti-war and civil rights demonstrators during the 1968 Democratic Convention.

The first black Chicago mayor was Democrat Harold Washington, victorious in 1979 by uniting his race with Hispanics and the white "Lakefront Liberals."

Plummeting approval ratings confined Mayor Lori Lightfoot, the architect of an investigation into the Henyard administration, to one term helming The Windy City. An attorney, she was the first avowed lesbian black woman in the nation to serve as mayor of a major municipality. Crime rates soared on her watch in the aftermath of the George Floyd killing. Lightfoot's decision to have a Christopher Columbus statue removed from a park and implementing an embargo on white reporters at press briefings compromised her popularity.

Leftist Brandon Johnson is the current mayor of Chicago. Enjoying teachers' and labor union endorsements, he defeated tough-on-crime candidate Paul Vallas for the seat, meeting the following day with fellow Democrats, Governor Pritzker and Attorney General Raoul, to strategize his tenure. He was instrumental in bringing the 2024 Democratic National Convention to Chicago. One of his appointees to the Chicago Board of Education, Reverend Mitchell Ikenna Johnson, inconvenienced the mayor following the Oct. 7 massacre with antisemitic social media posts unearthed from the past by critics.

In April of 2023, packs of teenagers and young adults committed a spree of vandalism and shootings in pivotal locations of the city, eliciting a lukewarm, forgiving response from Mayor Johnson:

"…in no way do I condone the destructive activity we saw in the Loop and lakefront this weekend. It is unacceptable and has no place in our city. However, it is not constructive to demonize youth who have otherwise been starved of opportunities in their own communities."

At last check, the 48-year-old mayor's approval ratings were abysmal.

The big picture implying grave repercussions for Thornton Township and the Village of Dolton regarding Supermayor Tiffany A. Henyard was painted in a letter to the Lansing Journal:

"There are two things I things I see wrong in contemporary American politics. The first issue is a lack of political awareness. Not just understanding the common function of how government works, but the historical view of how our current situation is caused by events that happened in the past. This leads to the second issue, and probably the biggest—the lack of accountability from the people. We vote people into office without considering their record. We refuse to evaluate their ability to even execute the duties of the office. We mainly vote by popularity and choose the lesser of two evils. Unfortunately, the local politics of the Southland is not immune to this epidemic.

For nearly three years, Thornton Township has spiraled into political turmoil. With the passing of longtime Supervisor Frank Zuccarelli and the appointment of Tiffany Henyard in March of 2022, the township has not seen this much attention in quite some time. With most of it being negative, the focus has been mostly on Henyard. Henyard, who is also the mayor of Dolton, has been accused of several unethical decisions and possible charges of corruption. These charges not only apply to her role as supervisor but as the mayor of Dolton as well.

Henyard comes from a long line of problematic politicians that has plagued the village of Dolton for nearly three decades. The last three decades saw several politicians in the village mismanage the resources of the town. The political career of Henyard started in 2013 when she was elected trustee under then-mayor Riley Rogers. While both Henyard and Rogers seemed like ideal politicians at the time, they unfortunately set back the village in their time in office. Marred by infighting and several economic decisions that almost led them to the verge of bankruptcy, Henyard was part of a government that failed to progress.

During Tiffany Henyard's time as Dolton trustee, many issues of the village were blamed on Rogers. This gave Henyard a golden opportunity to make her run for mayor in 2021, which she won. However, this is where the political blind spot comes into play. While Rogers was held accountable for some of the decisions he made as mayor, Henyard was able to slide under the radar. Her actions as a trustee were overlooked by her supporters. She verbally fought with Rogers and his supporters on the board. Very few saw her as chaotic. Instead of trying to achieve a consensus with the government, she was more antagonistic in her behavior. Henyard's personal record was also ignored. Public records show she was arrested in 2016 for criminal trespass. In 2019, CBS2 uncovered an investigation where Henyard severely neglected a property she owned and leased to a Section 8 renter. These things are just a few examples of how none of this was considered with the voters. Her supporters during the time pushed her to the front despite her questionable past.

Henyard's appointment to the supervisor of the township also comes with a lack of political awareness. Trustee Chris Gonzalez was the one who nominated Tiffany Henyard and voted for her along with Trustees Darlene Gray Everett and Jerry Jones. When the Lansing Journal interviewed Gonzalez on March 12, 2024, about why he nominated her, Gonzalez responded with his reason of her being young and a woman. He admitted that he did not know about the conflict she was having with the board in Dolton. Gonzalez's failure to vet Tiffany is an example of his disregard for protecting the interest of the township. And even though he would minimize it as a mistake, it is one that the township is paying for. While many who support his efforts for re-election would forgive him because he stands against the supervisor now, their lack of holding him accountable for his pivotal actions demonstrates the lack of political awareness among the people.

Mayor Michael Bilandic lost his re-election bid for mayor of Chicago in 1979 because of a mistake he made of not deploying enough snowplows during a huge blizzard earlier that year. Several political analysts attributed Donald Trump's failure to be re-elected in 2020 because of mistakes he made in his handling of the Covid-19 outbreak. These are a few examples of how voters felt about a mistake. These types of mistakes cost thousands of lives and billions of dollars. Those who have ushered Tiffany Henyard into her executive positions at the village and township have cost both municipalities several millions of dollars and utter chaos. If we're to hold Tiffany Henyard accountable, let us hold those people who helped her, both past and present, responsible for this mayhem."

Gardis Watts

Twenty-year resident of South Holland

Former Senior System Administrator for Thornton Township

Hearing comments made at a meeting about her Section 8 dwelling by the former president of the south suburban NAACP, relevant operatives should have intercepted Trustee Tiffany Henyard before it was too late.

"The kids got sick, their clothes got mold on it. There's termites in the house. There's feces under the house. The place is unlivable," said David Lowrey, Jr., who vowed to investigate with possible legal options.

The aloof Henyard stared smugly at him with a glint in her eyes as he addressed the board.

Podcaster AG Tactical believes few people, however, are swayed by her hapless, certifiably crazy snow shoveling in the middle of the night.

"Jedidiah (Brown) is on her head top, AG Tactical is on her head top, Cooking With Frank is on her head top—everybody's on her fucking head top right now, so she needs positive press, right?"

With her nostrils flaring and "bubble" eyes, according to AG Tactical's analysis of video, the bundled-up Tiff-Tiff shrieks "Hey guys, this is your Supermayor, Tiffany A. Henyard, the people's mayor," as two men navigate the light dusting over her shoulder.

The look on her face, he submits, is reminiscent of Jack Nicholson in "The Shining," screaming "Heeerrrrrre's Johnny!!!"

"If I saw her at night, it would scare me," AG Tactical says, noting that Halloween could be the best haven for her wackiness by wearing "a pink beanie and any dress over $2,000 that makes you look like a fuckin' moron."

"They (detractors) don't walk my walk," the Supermayor boasts. "If you signed up for this snow shoveling program, we will get to you shortly," claiming that she not only clears driveways, but streets.

AG Tactical threads imply a berserk woman addicted to snow.

"She is shoving her mother drive way"

"Cocaine is a hell of drug"

"Say no to drugs kids"

"She's got a crew all right! The Midnight Cocaine Train!"

"She is obviously stoned!"

"They're on the crack, man"

"YEAH. SHE'S SHOVELING SNOW...WINK WINK"

Speaking of driveways, Henyard wasted taxpayers' bling rumored to be $561,000 on replacing her mother's that accommodated a new Range Rover, inciting internet insurrection:

"This is pay for play corruption at its finest. What they do is, give the jobs to friends & family and get kickbacks."

"You mean $40000 driveway and $521,000 laundered through the system and put in her pocket allegedly."

"Her mother probably needed a new driveway, so Henyard put together a scheme to do many residents driveways, so it looks like it's on the up and up, but it was most likely so her mother can get a free driveway."

"I don't care what poison people put out there," the Supermayor proclaimed. "Y'all live here; they don't. The internet and the people, especially at my board meetings, can say whatever. But at the end of the day, we grew here, they flew here."

Attempting to dissuade anyone from challenging her at the polls, the haughty Henyard hatched an ordinance to lower the starting salary for township supervisor from nearly $250,000 to $25,000.

CHAPTER III: THE HENYARD GANG

It was not uncommon for Dolton and Thornton Township motorists to witness a veritable fleet of fancy, black SUV's zipping through traffic with Supermayor Tiffany A. Henyard and her lackeys in tow. In a village with a relatively high crime rate strapped for police officers, Henyard assembled a security detail worthy of Governor Pritzker or Chicago Mayor Brandon Johnson. Several police officers escorted her daily to meetings in both jurisdictions, special events, door-to-door canvassing, restaurants, and shopping that emitted total disdain for the taxpayers. A police officer was often assigned to her residence for overnight protection. Additional officers were present at meetings as residents scrambled to participate in public comments amid Henyard's vacillating attacks and indifference. They sometimes accompanied her on trips out of town.

The arrangement was costly, accruing over $1 million in overtime pay for her handpicked sycophants. Deputy Chief Lacey, known for punking unruly residents in meetings at Henyard's behest, reportedly earned more from OT (around $200,000) than his base salary in one year. Officer Terry Young absurdly accrued 303 hours of pay in two weeks.

"Some people take it as glamorous by having a bunch of police officers around and you being escorted and driven around," Riley Rogers said. "I never had a security detail as mayor."

Thanks to resistance from the trustees, three leased Tahoes and one Expedition were returned to the dealership. According to Trustee Kiana Belcher, the idiocy would have drained $718,000 from village coffers.

"You puttin' on a show. I don't know what you're talkin' about," Henyard rebelled when Belcher publicly raised the issue.

Belcher reacted curtly: "No, it's simple math."

Such insolence resulted in the removal of Belcher's picture from Village Hall. The trustee settled the score by displaying the photo at her table during meetings.

Former Police Chief Robert Collins sued Henyard for wrongful dismissal, saying the security force was unnecessary and that his wife's friendship with one of the mayor's political rivals instigated termination.

Collins, who landed on his feet in Florida as a chief, likened the officers to personal valets doing errands. Lacey catapulted to chief when he departed.

Collins found himself at the crux of a wrongful death lawsuit filed on behalf of Alexis Wilson, 19, who was fatally shot by Dolton police shortly after Henyard became mayor. The village settled for $900,000 without admitting fault. Collins released bodycam and restaurant surveillance video showing Wilson striking a drive-through window with a metal pipe. Wilson, claiming she was nude, refused when officers asked her to exit the car. A pursuit culminated in the shooting. Investigators recovered a semi-automatic weapon with an extended magazine in the vehicle.

Henyard initially condoned the actions of the officers, then apologized for the calamity when there was a demonstration outside her home. The case was brought up in meetings by residents already fuming at the fledgling Supermayor.

"Chief Collins was more of an ethically moral man," conceded Jedidiah Brown, the investigative operative in the trenches of Dolton and Thornton Township.

Brown clashed with Henyard and her gang on numerous occasions. In his interview with Hannibal Is Hungry, Brown said he was encouraged by local law enforcement sources and other officials to probe the possible sexual assault involving Dolton Trustee Andrew Holmes and Mayor Henyard's assistant Fenia Dukes in Las Vegas.

The well-known Chicago-bred social activist and now self-described investigative advocate, however, broadened the girth of his endeavor to expose other potential crimes and malfeasance. His primary residence today, a Texas apartment, resembles a television studio.

He mentioned being further emboldened by the determination of "content creators and You tubers. We (my team) are gonna give you guys (podcasters) information. And you are going to see us continue to keep the pressure and keep them uncomfortable until there is an arrest, a resignation, or the people voting differently. This thing is worldwide."

Hannibal Is Hungry lobbed a battery of questions at Brown: "This is the Democrat machine in Illinois on display," said the activist, chastising Cook as the most corrupt county in the nation while admitting he and his antagonists probably never figured a little town would become the epicenter. "You can tell greed has gotten in where they've done too much. They think there is honor among thieves."

He elaborated: "These (the Henyard disciples) are sociopaths—narcissistic people. These are ghetto-ass people. They think people are afraid. They're enriching their individual, personal lives and their friends. They literally think they are going to use street tactics with government power and they're just not smart enough."

According to Brown, one affront employed by Henyard, her main squeeze Kamal Woods, and Lacey, was trailing him into another township village driving an unmarked vehicle.

"So right now I'm being followed by a black car and he's pulling behind me," says Brown, visually and verbally phone recording live on Facebook.

Leaning out the window, Brown treats them to a few salty words as the vehicle starts pulling away:

"I'm not fuckin' afraid."

"Stop playin' with me. Play with yo momma."

"You got the gun and the badge. Get your bitch out if you gonna do this, clown."

"Ain't nobody scared of you whole-ass nigger."

"Shouldn't you be in Dolton?"

Brown turns the tables by following the trio. At some point, Henyard calls the local police, claiming they were on a shopping trip for her daughter. Lacey, sporting an N.Y.P.D T-shirt, tells the responding officer Brown was the aggressor, trying to block them in at a convenience store. Woods says they were merely attempting to protect Henyard in reporting Brown. "I know I have her in the car. That's my woman."

When asked by police whether he knew the supposed assailant, Woods says yes, that "I recognize him out of a crowd of people. (Brown) get on the internet just blastin' and talkin' about your business."

No charges were filed in connection with the incident.

"Kamal is the boss. He is the guy who is in charge," determines Brown, informing Hannibal Is Hungry that Woods was behind the thuggish Nino Brown spectacle at a meeting, clandestine dealings, roughhousing businesses, and that Henyard is no stranger to sleeping with married men. "He is the guy steering the ship because he is drilling the boss."

Saying the "biggest help (in life) comes from above," with religious connotations, Woods was recorded waxing philosophically about troubled people needing to seek help: "You can give them the experience of that you hope for and pray for when you were born, from the moment of abandonment, long suffering, stress, PTSD (Post Traumatic Stress Syndrome), all the difficult things that amount to trauma that you feel from different angles in your life."

The less doting Woods, aka "Leotis" and "Cigarette Break" courtesy of Cooking With Frank, lurked in the corner of meetings attired for a street corner hustle or back-alley thuggery, slouching and staring menacingly at citizens launching opinions deviating from the predilections of his lover, Supermayor Tiffany A. Henyard.

It is debatable, though, whether he scared a burly, explicitly irate man with an animated speaking style at the podium who said he had been watching "as this village is being run into the ground by this woman." He claimed she did the same to the township and his alma mater, South Suburban College. "I take all of these things very personally. One of your trustees assaulted a woman. He (Andrew Holmes) belongs in jail along with you, Miss Henyard, and your wigs," he said prior to storming out as police officers closed in.

For clarification, Henyard reneged on paying the lease for her hamburger restaurant at the school.

Hannibal Is Hungry provides a comprehensive mission statement with a strong fiscal component that poignantly rings true for Supermayor Henyard's victims:

"We are dedicated to uncovering scams in the realms of money, media and society. Our channel is your go-to source for revealing the hidden truths and deceptions that impact our daily lives. We're not just about exposing the bad; we also delve into financial insight and social commentary to keep you informed and empowered. Whether you're seeking to safeguard your finances or stay ahead in a world of scams, hit that Subscribe button. Join us in our mission to unveil the real stories behind the headlines."

Hannibal Is Hungry summarizes the burgeoning momentum against Henyard and her associates in his terse critique of a meeting halfway through her tumultuous tour as mayor:

"It was Tiffany Henyard being completely cooked. They said everything they wanted to say to her face, calling her dumb, she can't read, she can't speak, she can't write, and her grammar's terrible."

One female resident castigates Henyard and warns of her collapse: "Pay for your own makeup and your own style. You are so stupid. You doing pay to play. The FBI know—they know everything you doin'. And baby, you better come up with those receipts."

Unrelenting Henyard detractor Mary Avent is livid:

"Mr. (Michael) Del Galdo (village attorney) unass that seat. You got a million point two (dollars) between us and the township. You can go home and play with your checkbook or whatever you play with—but sittin' up there, you don't protect us. You represent the mayor against the people's trustees. What kind of bullshit is that? And you call yourself a lawyer? It tells me what you think of us. And the same with you Keith (Keith Freeman, the village and township administrator). The nerve of y'all to put your asses in front of us when you disrespect us."

At one juncture, the Del Galdo firm threatened to cease counseling the village because it was not being paid. A partner, Tiffany Nelson-Jaworski, began handling Dolton legal matters in place of Del Galdo himself.

Another tirade is consummated by the formally attired Alicia Nichole whose articulation and familiarity with the language dwarf Henyard and her companions combined, and specifically refers to the caustic recent scenario engrossing Jedidiah Brown:

"You always said 'let me educate y'all.' What are your credentials? You don't have the wherewithal to educate a preschooler. It is insane. Please retire that phrase. You're not accountable. You don't respect people that have a different opinion. You're not qualified. We're not even going to talk about the grammar—that's embarrassing. Keith Freeman—let me not forget about that deer in the headlights look on the news. I hope you get everything coming to you. Chief Lacey—you're bogus. I saw the whole live (Facebook feed) with Jedidiah. You literally concocted a story, and you went and made a report based on your imagination—what you said did not happen. He was live and people were watching live. I can't understand why you would so blatantly, knowing your position, knowing the oath you are sworn to, disrespect for no reason other than a personal reason, not a legal reason."

Tiff-Tiff, emblazoned in brighter colors at the meeting than a peacock, honors tradition by staring vacantly at the table, barely acceding to the speakers.

Cooking With Frank says she doodles while others express themselves:

Take All Da Monee

Hyre Louis (Lacey)

Kill Stan (Stanley Brown)

My BOO Leotis (Kamal Woods)

Stacking up Likes, Hannibal Is Hungry wonders what depravity lies ahead in the surreal saga of Supermayor Tiffany Henyard.

Jedidiah Brown, who bonded around the cause with Hannibal Is Hungry in their interview, spent a night in jail after concluding his public comments at a Dolton board meeting by confronting Trustee Andrews Holmes about Fenia Dukes.

"So, I'm simply asking you right now because we sittin' here looking at your face. I'm utterly disgusted. There's a woman with a child waiting for a response from you. Was it consensual or was it not? Did you rape that woman? Did you put something in her drink? And damn it, you gonna answer, and you gonna answer me. I promise you that."

The lean, scrappy investigative advocate, attired in a black ball cap and Chi-Southside light jacket with pinstripes, abandoned the lectern and briskly walked across the floor toward the older Holmes, who reacted by leaping out of his seat to move in Brown's direction. Police officers intervened before punches were thrown as the venue once again devolved into bedlam.

While no charges emerged from the ordeal in Las Vegas, a lawsuit against Holmes by Dukes's attorney was initiated when a tape leaked of the trustee boasting to Dolton cop Byron Miles on the trip about having the woman in his room. Passages from the lawsuit indicated Holmes, apparently reveling in his "conquest," panned a cell phone video camera near the partially dressed woman, targeted private anatomy, and lecherously removed articles of clothing from her body.

Dukes challenged the motionless, reticent Holmes at a meeting: "I'm going to talk to you myself. Why did you do that? And if I'm lyin', all these people right here, all the cameras, (the mayor), all these people. Tell them I'm lyin' then. Is that why you never said anything, is that why you disappeared as soon as this came out, is that why? I'm supposed to be scared of you?"

The officer who witnessed the invasive video was demoted from the Supermayor's disgraceful security detail; Las Vegas police did not arrest Trustee Holmes for lack of evidence that an actual assault occurred. Dukes approached Henyard after the trip with her story, feeling confident the mayor would assist meaningfully because of their personal rapport. Dukes said the mayor (serially prone to thinking selfishly) was mostly worried about preserving her political prospects. Shortly thereafter, Henyard arbitrarily terminated Dukes who, like many other former employees, sued for personal retaliation.

Dolton Trustee Tammie Brown disparaged the Supermayor:

"How could you live with yourself? How? That's somebody's daughter. I couldn't live with myself even knowing that something like that happened and I didn't say anything about it. This happened on your watch. You have a daughter."

"I'm appalled. For someone to have the leader in our community that always speaks on black women to cover up something like this is outrageous," Trustee Kiana Belcher said. "I'm furious."

The Illinois Department of Human Rights launched an investigation that apparently yielded no significant outcome.

Henyard's hateful high crimes and hijinks paralleled other devious scoundrels, according to reader comments with political overtones at the New York Post newspaper:

"Fanni Willis wannabe."

"She got Jussie Smollett's endorsement."

"nobody should feel sorry for the citizens that voted her in. enjoy your vote. I know everyone else is."

"Another DEI success story!"

"The apocalypse gets closer every day..."

"Thank you, Lord for letting me live somewhere other than there."

"Why do people always automatically assume that someone who behaves badly suffers from mental illness? How about someone is just a selfish, greedy, bad person?"

"It's Illinois. Democrats there just as corrupt as those in New Jersey."

"Dolton is one of a bunch of towns right on the edges of Chicago that are broke and in a dangerous state of disrepair. These towns are all democratic run health hazards."

Internet consensus advanced the precept that Democrats pander to deadbeats, misfits, and criminals.

Despite bleak perspectives suggesting ruthlessly parasitic, lawless exploitation by Henyard and her flunkeys of Dolton and Thornton Township with alarming consequences, the Supermayor was sworn in as director at large of the National Black Caucus of Elected Officials in October of 2023, allegedly seeking "to bring about positive change and impact communities by influencing policy, sharing knowledge, and fostering collaboration among African-American leaders within the National League of Cities."

More incredibly, perhaps, boyfriend Kamal "Leotis" Woods wore a formal blue suit to the proceedings.

Two regulars at township meetings were catatonic lawyer Eric Stach, another Del Galdo retread and the object of relatively innocuous joking on the internet, and Clerk Loretta Wells, whose affable hugs and chats with the bonkers Henyard were unsettling.

"How creepy is that lawyer next to Tiffany? Is he even human?"

"(Stach) sits there with the same expression on his face," Cooking With Frank says. "The only thing you see him do is blink."

"(Wells) is team Tiffany all the way," surmises Just Doing Nails, observing that her records-taking intentionally omits "Carliar" spoken by Henyard to avoid incrimination. "She's been more biased toward Tiffany Henyard."

Just Doing Nails says Wells's last-minute attempt to abscond electoral board duties galvanizes the liability that her reputation for pleasing the Supermayor has become.

"Dear Judge,

I, Loretta Wells, am writing to you to request that I be removed from the Thornton Township Electoral Board. I know as clerk of the township, it is my obligation to serve on the board, but I believe that outside public members because of their knowledge and expertise, would best serve on this board. Plus, I am physically and mentally exhausted due to the dysfunction within our township and daily responsibilities as the Township Clerk.

I beg you to please consider removing me as a member of the Township Electoral Board.

Thank you."

Loretta Wells

Clerk, Thornton Township

Circuit Judge Maureen Ward Kirby denied her request.

Cyber sentiments are damning:

"I wonder if the FEDS spoke to Clerk Wells."

"Clerk Wells is running. She should have run months ago."

"She needs to go down when Tiffany does even if she is trying to quit!!! She has been abetting Tiffany's behavior and actions for 3 years!"

"The clerk doesn't want to be on a losing team. Plus she must know a lot more than she is telling."

Her husband Terry, the Village of Phoenix mayor, became the chairman of South Suburban College Board of Directors when Zuccarelli died.

"I don't think the people trust you anymore," Sheriff Frank tells Clerk Wells. "We done had our eye on you for a minute. Remember when Carmen Carlisle tried to call in and do her duty even though there was a restraining order against Keithopotamus Price? And you and Tiffany Hentard was whisperin'—you, Tiffany Hentard, and Darlene Gray Everett."

Carlisle obtained the order over concerns about her personal safety for speaking out against the Henyard administration.

In meeting minutes, according to resident Jennifer Robertz, Wells funneled a motion to approve a baseless Supermayor tax refund without the lawful voting quorum. In addition, her township web page featured a graphic of the FOIA (Freedom of Information Act) that the Henyard regime brazenly ignored, and pictures of them warmly coalescing.

Chawanne Burns rides with the Podcaster Posse while professing conservative inclinations and versatility in her lengthy mission statement, an indication that the platform attracts an array of fans.

Hello All,

"I'm Chawanne Burns and welcome to your go-to source for credit business, and controversial politics from a conservative standpoint. Here, we discuss the ins and outs of business credit while also diving into the controversial world of politics, providing you with a fresh, conservative perspective on today's most pressing issues. My channel is dedicated to providing well-researched, balanced, and insightful content on credit, business and politics. We aim to foster open-minded discussions and encourage healthy debate while exploring conservative point of view on various political issues.

Subscribe today and let's explore these topics together."

In this episode, Burns exposes information alleging nepotism and cronyism perpetrated by Supermayor Henyard in both Thornton Township and the Village of Dolton and derides her unsavory morals, particularly the dalliance with Kamal "Cigarette Break" Woods.

"This fool (Woods) is married. So, she's sleepin' with a married man. This is the type of person Tiffany Henyard is. She deals with thugs, and she sleeps with married men. Does she have good judgement? No, she doesn't. (Tiffany) you love criminals. You love thugs to do your bidding. You guys (the audience) let me know, am I being too harsh?"

Instantaneous listener response: "How in the world is she claiming someone else's husband? This beyond a narcissist!?!?"

She reminds her loyalists that Henyard was jailed in 2016 for busting into cars. "We should be doin' background checks on individuals. She's a thief. She went from pet thievin' to big crime."

As for Woods, she says he earns over $100,000 annually managing a program for youths. "I don't know what skills he has. It's crazy," Burns says.

The state reportedly doubled its grant for youth initiatives at the township, partially squandered at a youth summit where Henyard stole center stage as always; rest assured, no one confused her with Whitney Houston when she belted out a note or two.

The podcaster is peeved:

"Why are you doin' that? Why are you torturing people? And you tryin' to sing!?"

A video clip is shown of Supermayor Henyard regaling her man: "I'm a single parent. Kamal has changed our all's life. He has been nothing but a loving father to my child. Thank God for Kamal!" Burns says that Kamal, running a clothing business in Glenwood and a Dolton car wash that is delinquent paying property taxes, just refinanced a home with his wife in the Village of South Holland.

Woods, meanwhile, resides with the Supermayor and her daughter in Dolton, "lyin' and confusin' the little girl. What kind of ghetto ass shit is that?" Burns conjectures. He also owed child support stemming from a prior relationship.

Kamal's name is one letter short of Kamala, the presidential candidate Burns skewers in numerous episodes.

Complicating the debauchery, Burns says, is a custody battle between Henyard and the child's biological father, Early Walker, now married to someone else, and the owner of a towing company that allegedly received a contract for services without a competitive bidding process.

A rival towing proprietor noted that Henyard, Walker, Stanley Brown, Robert Hunt, and Michael Smith were all friends.

"Need to interview baby daddy," a follower posts.

Caustic cronyism and gnarly nepotism allegedly submerge the village and the township.

Burns's viewers learn that William Moore, a vehement Henyard disciple, directs housing and permitting in Dolton while working administratively at the township along with his wife. Stanley Brown, seemingly obligated to vote with the Supermayor and nicknamed "Blue Black Brown," and the "Brown Hornet" for a cartoon character by Cooking With Frank, holds trustee and director of community outreach township positions. A subdued Henyard supporter Jerry Jones, who started waffling and resigned as a township trustee, is the Village of Dolton water department boss. Jones's resignation, according to sources, was spurred when his son enraged his superior, township food pantry director and gargantuan Henyard goon Keith Price, for saying mice were creating unsanitary conditions. The Supermayor's sister-in-law, Rosie

Henyard, operates township youth and family services while her cousin, Tamika Henyard, manages senior services. Topping off the circus ring of cozy insularity, personal Tiff-Tiff hairstylist, Tyreshia Butler, is a case worker and outreach specialist.

"You got to be a piece of shit woman," Burns blurts as the podcast winds down.

An audience member wonders: "Where u see (Henyard's) future going? Prison or out of office?" Maybe both.

Cooking With Frank rolls video of Early Walker engaging children at a lemonade stand raising money for St. Jude Children's Research Hospital with hopes of attending the upcoming Chicago Sky-Indiana Fever game. He humorously predicts they will be Caitlin Clark, rather than Angel Reese fans, by the time the final buzzer sounds.

"Shout out to Early. He kicked Tiffany Henyard ass to the curb," Frank says. "Got him a good wife (a television news anchor), and he livin' a good life. Sounds like God is on Early's side, not (Tiffany's)."

"Craving insightful narratives that mainstream channels often ignore? Want news that genuinely shapes your world, from societal tensions to crime trends? Welcome to 'News For Reasonable People.' Your host Reynolds—a keen business owner—and socially aware citizen —brings you a balanced and perceptive daily breakdown of the issues that matter. Experience in-depth reports, live streams that pique your curiosity (but you'd rather not visit), and exclusive interviews and documentation that other outlets avoid. To stay updated, subscribe and activate the notification bell—you won't want to miss a moment of our compelling episodes."

Reynolds delivers coherently in relatable lay terms from Seattle with a dark brick backdrop.

"We got at least two videos to come out each week that you won't see anywhere else. Here's an example (this is for member content only): New York City robbery turns into deadly fight. You had a guy who was getting basically mugged on a New York subway and he killed two of the robbers. You're not hearing about that on mainstream media, are you?"

Primary reasons for why people enjoy podcasts are delineated:

The Intimacy of Audio

At the heart of podcasting's appeal is the sense of intimacy it creates. Audio is uniquely personal. An individual often consumes podcasts through headphones, creating a one-to-once connection with the host. The atmosphere forges a bond akin to friendship, producing loyal and dedicated listening habits.

The Power of Storytelling

Humans are natural story tellers. Podcasts provide a narrative form that our brains are wired to engage. Information processed into stories is more likely to be remembered and recommended, playing into the innate desire for weaving yarns.

Convenience and Multitasking

In a fast-paced world, podcasts offer the perfect multitasking companion. They fit seamlessly into daily routines—during commutes, workouts, or chores—aligning with the psychological principle of economizing action. Lives are enriched through entertainment and learning without having to allocate special time for them.

Niche Interest and Personal Growth

Podcasts cater to a wide range of human interests, from the mainstream to the esoteric. This opportunity to "find your tribe" satisfies a listener's search for identity and community. Furthermore, podcasts satiate a psychological quest for personal growth, cultivating self-improvement content in a digestible format.

Control and Choice

The on-demand nature of podcasting enhances audience province over what, when, and how they listen, enabling their autonomy. This power of choice is psychologically gratifying, fostering a sense of self-efficacy and independence in the media consumption process.

The Para-social Relationship

Podcast followers frequently develop rapport with hosts, feeling as if they know them on a personal level. This perceived relationship, while potentially one-sided, is strong and emotionally fulfilling for human beings requiring social interaction and affirmation.

Continuity and Routine

Listeners incorporate specific podcasts into their daily or weekly patterns, creating a comforting, reassuring sense of consistent predictability. Regular podcast platforms provide refuge and structure for people in our sometimes confusing and frenetic lives.

The Community Aspect

Podcasts extend into offline and online communities where participants merge interests and perspectives. This social aspect embraces the psychological penchant for belonging. Podcast enthusiasts discuss the challenges of the day, adhering to a larger collective.

Escapism and Relaxation

Many listeners rely on podcasts as an avenue for momentary escape, desperate for relief from daily stress. The immersive experience is a calming mental and even therapeutic diversion.

Learning and Cognitive Engagement

Educational podcasts embrace the inherent human curiosity and pleasure derived from learning. Cognitive coalescence stimulates our quest for knowledge and intellectual growth.

The psychology of podcasting is complex, rooted in fundamental human behaviors and tendencies. Understanding these psychological elements is important to podcasters crafting content that marries the intrinsic needs of their listeners. The popularity of podcasts relies upon savvy practitioners to maximize this intimate, flexible, and community-oriented medium exploring the far reaches of cyberspace.

Podcasters reserved front row seats for the greatest show on Earth as demonstrated by a flurry of dumbfounded citizens' threads obliterating the mayor on Hannibal Is Hungry from various locations:

"I live in Kansas and I'm so invested in this. I pray she and her henchmen are held liable for their deeds that injured the town. The nation is watching!!!"

"I live in Australia. I don't know how I found myself down this rabbit hole. I am truly shocked by what is happening."

"I am in Texas this is so entertaining. I being following this for a few weeks. I love the fact that the people exposing the mayor are black so she's can't claim racism."

"It isn't any wonder this country's moral is going down like a leaded balloon with these kind of people in control. What ever happened to professionalism, self-respect and protocol."

"I'm all the way in Florida and even I can see they goin' to 'SUPER JAIL.'"

"We have a mayor in London very similar."

"The towns people have support from other states too."

"Grew up there (Dolton) on Clark St. Never thought I would see my hometown village embarrassed nationally like this. I stand with the residents fighting this corruption."

"Hannibal you do an amazing job following this corruption. Keep it up my friend. NOTE: the meetings are one punch away from this looking like Iraqi Parliament."

"Listen, anyone with a wisp of dignity would have resigned after such monumental public trashing."

"This is what happens when you put thugs in office. Never seen a mayor get into a shouting match with a citizen. How does someone like this get elected?"

"This is a MESS!"

"Lemme educate y'all, lemme educate y'all. I AM WEAK."

"Tiffany Henyard actually had the audacity to claim that 'y'all are being hoodwinked, bamboozled, and led astray with fake information.' Yes, that's true, and SHE is the one who is doing it."

"Her outfit says 'HEY LOOK AT ME! LISTEN TO ME! IGNORE EVERYONE ELSE.'"

"Every community ought to be able to express their thoughts without any comments or retorts from the government."

"I want to buy trustee (Kiana) Belcher lunch/dinner. I love this woman"

"Dolton is a bad representation of black people in power."

"These meetings are like a Netflix series, I can't wait for the next episode."

"That was awesome. All those people got to tell Henyard to her face —without interruption—what we have been screaming at our computer screens for weeks."

"Thanks to social media, most of the world knows the adventure of Tiff and Dolton."

Worried Dolton Trustee Brittney Norwood was quoted by the Atlanta Black Star: "I feel as if I'm living in a dictatorship. I'm always in disbelief. I always pray before I get to the meetings, and I pray for (Henyard) that she's changed. I think the residents should know that she is manipulative. I want them to understand that we are fighting for what's right."

"You want to sit there and put us down for doing our job," Clerk Alison Key said. "We don't have to put up a fake video. We do everything from our heart."

Impervious to laws, statutes, rules, regulations, and other impediments to power, Henyard brusquely shuffled personnel and appointments with impunity. For example, at one juncture she tried to supplant Administrator Keith Freeman, facing bankruptcy fraud charges and suspected of cooperating with the FBI probe, and Chief Lacey, also scrambling from bankruptcy allegations and losing his law enforcement certification, by circumventing the trustees.

CHAPTER IV: HOT ON THE TRAIL

Illinois Leaks reported Lacey was stripped of his badge and owning firearms as a condition of being granted bail in the federal case. At first, Henyard stubbornly retained Lacey, who threatened officers with insubordination if they did not submit to his directives. Eventually, however, the department voted no confidence in Lacey, his service weapon was seized, and the village fired him in August of 2024.

The Supermayor attacked Cooking With Frank for relishing the downfall of Keith Freeman and "Lethargic" Lewis Lacey:

"Frank how bout you pay me because majority of yo channel is a smear campaign on my name for what…clickbait. You owe me a check frank and I WILL be suing you for defamation of character when after I will win all these lawsuits. I GOT ALL THE RECEIPTS"

Frank tosses her in the frying pan:

"You got more important things to do henYARD lol, like make sure you stay out of prison. Ya homies are all going down and your time is coming shortly after that henYARD"

AG Tactical studies a deposition by Freeman characterizing the situation at the Village of Dolton as "chaos." Foggy statements indicate he was previously administrator for the Thorton Township villages of Robbins and Phoenix, could not remember the year of his high school graduation, and earned a "business certificate" from Mount Mercy College in Cedar Rapids, Iowa, for two part-time semesters.

Henyard's "right hand man," according to AG Tactical, "got a few amenities, got a few escort rides—he said, 'Oh, I like this,'" noting that the Supermayor and her administrator always "distance" themselves from fiscal accountability.

Listeners are not fond of Freeman, who intercepted a Chicago television crew trying to tail her highness:

"Kieth ripped off another city. He's a criminal and a scammer."

"The fact he had file bankruptcy 2x is not a sign he knows finances."

"There's a reason they call him Thief freeman because he's a slithering buffoon, the fact that he's most likely thinking of ways to weasel himself out of any criminal charges by turning on Tahoe tiff, shows there is no honor among thieves."

The Actual Justice Warrior podcast, hosted by Sean Fitzgerald, profiles the Supermayor's hiring of Michael Smith for the position of administrator although Cook County Judge Thaddeus Wilson deemed Henyard's actions untenable.

Promoting his product while soliciting a "True" AJW subscription fee of $6 and $60 for elite "Truest" AJW memberships, Actual Justice Warrior says "I'm just a random guy talking about news, YouTube stuff, SJW's, and trying to have a little fun while doing it. Expect some reactions, sketches and other nonsense in the future."

Fitzgerald, flanked by a human skeleton, unveils this episode with "greetings and salutations" to the channel's listeners as his light-hearted tone evaporates in the pursuit of Henyard: "My name is Sean and today we're here to talk about an absolutely devastating blow to the Supermayor delivered by a court who sided with the board of trustees to say 'hey look, you cannot appoint your puppets without the consent of the board of trustees.'"

Actual Justice Warrior ignites a clip of Henyard lauding her new man Smith, Cooking With Frank's "Hunchback of Thornton Township."

"He have a wealth of great information. He's a young person. He knows the law like the back of his hand," Henyard gushes over Smith, who once ingeniously talked about connecting the "dotts" by spelling the word with two t's.

Actual Justice Warrior: "He is a guy with a checkered past, to say the least. It's actually hilarious that the Supermayor described him as someone who knows the law like the back of his hand because it may be unsurprising to the people in my audience, but surprising to some people thinking there has to be some bottom to the depth of corruption and insanity of the Supermayor."

According to Actual Justice Warrior, Smith has been convicted of domestic battery, and official misconduct in connection with stealing gasoline while impersonating a police officer when he was an elected official in the township Village of Dixmoor. "Honestly, that is one of the most ghetto things I have heard of in my entire life."

Fitzgerald recalls that Smith resigned from a deanship at a high school in the wake of accusations that he sexually harassed and groomed a student on social media, even accosting her 15-year-old boyfriend. "This is the guy she wants as her right-hand man—a criminal scumbag."

Podcast threads further the dialogue:

"We had a similar thing here in Australia. My town Auburn got a criminal mayor. He even had his criminal gang members come into town and stand over the other councilors with threats of violence."

"The ratchet mayor."

"Too bad the people elected a female rapper she will be gone soon embarrassing that city."

"If this woman wasn't black and the FBI wasn't compromised, she'd be in prison."

"Being black has nothing to do with being wrong. She is trying to gaslight an entire community for her corrupt acts."

"All this is hilarious. But until people go to jail, it's all meaningless. She has done her ghetto thing, and will move on."

"Someone tell Lil Wayne to take off that wig."

"This person single-handedly made me hate the expression y'all"

"If you can't navigate your native language after the better part of three decades, then you can't run a village's government."

"We have a constant pattern of her hiring people without doing a proper background check and presenting it to the board," Dolton Trustee Brittney Norwood lamented. "That's our issue. That could pose a great danger to our community."

"It's not a good feeling working in a hostile work environment," Trustee Tammie Brown said. "That verdict (by Judge Wilson) yesterday was good for the employees doing things the correct way, decent and in order. I'm happy and I also got calls from the residents, and they are happy as well."

Burt Odelson, the lawyer representing the trustees, asserted: "The board has been absolutely fantastic in trying to keep the government operating. The people suffer, the employees suffer while her reign of terror continues."

Henyard's personal attorney, Beau "Brisket" (a Cooking With Frank label) Brindley, retorted: "Mayor Henyard will appeal. And the truth will come out—a truth that reveals a corrupt board of trustees trying to hijack the mayor's office through false statements and outright criminal misconduct."

Reviews of Brindley mimicked his client, tallying a paltry 1.7 on the 5-point scale:

"Listening to him sit beside Tiffany Henyard and lie to defend her actions, when there are plenty of videos of Tiffany making statements of all her wrong doings. I hope his practice can be reviewed by the BAR."

"Dude accepted Tiffany Henyard as a client and somehow didn't expect EVERYONE to call him out…what a sucker, good luck getting paid."

"lol this is the only person tiffany can afford…embarrassing"

"BEWARE do not hire Beau B. Brindley, he's a very unpredictable person! A crook a liar a THIEF and he does not care for his clients!"

Actual Justice Warrior notes that one of Henyard's most frightening hires was code enforcement officer Lavelle Redmond, who spent 25 years in the clink for a gang rape and the barbaric beating of two teenaged girls.

"The fact is that she associates with corrupt criminal types, and that has been proven out time and time again by the people working in her administration," the Podcaster Posse deputy huffs.

Listeners appreciate the podcast and the hullabaloo's potential:

"Thank you for covering this like no one online or on tv!"

"Ah yes, the Village of Dolton. Someone should make a TV show out of this."

Laughing heartily, Chawanne Burns mocks the intimacy of the Supermayor's inner sanctum with a photo of Kamal Woods and Michael Smith standing next to one another.

"She used to date this dude (Smith) right here. He lookin' like a turtle, a dark turtle. Kamal ain't bad lookin' but you could tell he got those grey teeth so you know he smoke Newports. They dated the same person (Henyard)."

The aggrieved Supermayor, resenting media scrutiny and accusing Dolton trustees of "secret squirrel meetings," began the short-lived "On Tha Move" podcast in spring of 2024. The glamor glutton of Dolton and Thornton Township kicks off Episode 1/Truth Speaks with a close-up of her putting on makeup, donning a white evening gown and gold high heels, exuding artificial grace and elegance as she enters an opulent office, and finally spinning around 360 degrees in her "throne" to greet the audience.

Henyard's flirtation with refined royalty, though, vanishes when she introduces herself gleefully as a nervous, giggling teenager might do: "Hey guys! This is Sooooooopermayor Tiffany Henyard, the people's mayor! So, I heard you guys are looking for me!" Stale, piped-in applause emanates.

In the zenith of irony given the Henyard camp's upheaval over social media, "I saw it (announcing the inaugural Supermayor podcast) on the internet so it must be true," says a female with a hushed, albeit enticing voice as the segment opens.

"I'm gonna show you how and why fake news really do exist," Henyard harps while assaulting the English language and rehashing Malcolm X's idea that the media sometimes adjudicate an innocent person as guilty.

Echoing his comrades and warming up for "On Tha Move," Keith Price enlisted race to defend her:

"There's so much more than somebody just running around, spending all types of money. There's answers that's coming on the podcast. She'll start telling her story. But it saddens me that nothing has changed in all these years since Malcolm X talked about the ballot or the bullet. We have black people attacking black people when they won't say a thing to a Caucasian (presumably Frank Zuccarelli) when they are in the spot."

Republican Tim DeYoung, who worked for Zuccarelli, explained the Henyard dilemma to the Illinois Answers Project: "For the township and the administration now there's utter disrespect and disregard for the law. Everything is about patronage and who you are friends with now with Tiffany and her crew. Everything is all about her. Her only goal is to make herself look good."

For those who question why she commands multiple positions of authority, podcaster Tiffany says: "What do you mean I got two titles, hater? How you lettin' the losers tell the story? Stop listenin' to the losers because you gotta go talk to a winner so you know how to win. All we do is win (referencing her election, appointment, and combatting the inundation of lawsuits against her). Win no matter what. Twenty-five and oh, baby. Twenty-five to zero in my lawsuits."

The Supermayor's exaggerations were easily refuted while scores of litigation dockets floundered.

Irony abounded when Henyard, with her expansive collection of hair hats, was sued by barber Tyrone Isom, Jr., alleging that "a policy of choosing (and) denying applicants" for "financial and political reasons" scuttled his remodeled business.

"I was just chasing my tail, and as I was chasing my tail, my finances were wearing thin," Isom, Jr. said.

Henyard goes back to the identity well, mentioning Women's History Month and saying "y'all (female detractors) tryin' to tear me down. God ain't gonna let you. At the end of the day, I have been chosen. I sit in rooms and at tables with people that's just like me really uplifting community, uplifting women."

She lambasts a Chicago television station story about Dr. Nicole Scott, whose FREE-N-DEED grocery store catering to financially challenged Dolton residents was never sanctioned by the village. Scott, having purchased a dilapidated shopping center with space for the market, told the reporter that nearly all attempts to detail specifications and address concerns with officials were ignored. A belated notice from the village said: "As per your request, the (project) drawings DO NOT meet the necessary requirements for an effective plan review."

When asked whether it was another example of dysfunction in Dolton, Dr. Scott answered in the affirmative, saying the residents were the ultimate victims.

The Supermayor is adamant: "It starts wich (meaning with) you. I need you to call the company that did the inspection. Go fix the building. Show the people what you need to do," adding that the news station's rendition of what occurred was biased and deficient.

"I love y'all despite all the lies you told on me," says Henyard, ostensibly speaking to Dr. Scott and the collective. "I want to showcase that by saying my door's always open, but it's up to you to walk through it. Check your closet; clean your house; clean your mess!"

Podcast technicians furnish a video of Dr. Scott, probably with hopes on the horizon for the grocery, praising the Supermayor at an American

Association of Single Parents event: "We are in support of Supermayor Tiffany Henyard. She has amazing initiative and programs in the Southland for the community. We're glad to be walking alongside her to see the community change for the better."

Henyard harpoons the statement as disingenuous. "Come on lady, I told you, stop lying," basking in the chance to mock her.

The Supermayor also defends her crackdown on illegal after-hours clubs in Dolton that allegedly operate without business and liquor licenses, in some instances fronting illegal gambling. Video clips depict drunkenness and fighting as she assails the owners of at least two establishments who say they were harassed and shut down by police for not contributing to her political war chest.

"They just rushed in here. Put police at the front door like they were doing a raid on a drug house or something," remembered Sevone Garfield, the head of security at Pablo's Café and Bar.

Pablo's owner, George Mseeh, was shocked: "Everything going peacefully. Nothing going on. Like 10 police officers come in and they start pushing customers from here. And he said, 'if you don't leave, we're gonna lock you up.'"

Kumar Soni, proprietor of Rinky's Bar and Café, feared for his staff: "I have like 23 employees that work from the local township. And now at the end of the day, all the employees are going to lose their job."

"It's ridiculous. We all have mouths to feed. They're not giving us any explanation," security officer Andrea Thomas said.

Henyard was found in contempt of court after refusing to sign off on a liquor license for St. Patrick's, a three-story restaurant and banquet hall. The attorney for the business said, "It's been a challenge to put it mildly. It shouldn't be so difficult. This is an ordinary event to get liquor licenses issued."

The pre-Madonna "night owl" Supermayor showed up to the court hearing 30 minutes late. Asked point-blank by the judge whether she would render her signature, Henyard rebelled by talking spasmodically in circles, inviting the contempt edict.

With profoundly personal undercurrents, Henyard had gone "Jekyll and Hyde" since the groundbreaking for St. Patrick's: "I'm happy to announce that these two black African Americans—they're about to put up a upscale sit-down, full restaurant."

Unfazed by intrusions, her highness culminates the episode confidently: "I love you (the people) and there is nothin' you can do about it, even the hateful" with gentler, kinder elevator music playing softly.

As for internet supposition about her travails: "The world's watchin', but y'all don't live in our community to really know what's really goin' on."

Her "community," revolving around the two roles of supervisor and mayor, piqued a plea for Illinois government consolidation in a letter to the Shaw Local News Network:

"More township government shame, taxpayer-funded abuse and waste. Thornton Township Supervisor Tiffany Henyard, who is already under fire for spending public money promoting herself and township government, has her name and smiling face on four giant taxpayer funded billboards on Interstate 57 and Bishop Ford Expressway. Vinyl signs cost $10,000 and Clear Channel Outdoor Advertising's cost is $12,000 for one month. The township board was never consulted according to Thornton Township Trustee Chris Gonzalez. Henyard's picture and name is also on township vehicles, buildings, and even on rugs. Township Supervisor Henyard, who is part-time, makes $224,000 and is paid over $46,000 as the mayor of Dalton.

Illinois has 1,430 township governments, 1,391 township road districts, 334 multi-township assessment districts and 26 township cemetery districts. A total of 3,381 taxpayer opportunities of government corruption, cronyism, nepotism, patronage and waste! Most states do not have the township level of government as well. Government consolidation should start at the township level.

Illinois has thousands more units of government than any other state. The movement of Illinois residents to other states with fewer governments and lower taxes will not cease until the Illinois General Assembly makes government consolidation a priority!

I can say, without hesitation, that Illinoisans are fed up spending their hard earned dollars on supporting extra layers of overlapping governments and the funding of their officials, employees, benefits, buildings, machinery, equipment, vehicles, and overhead."

Bob Anderson

Wonder Lake

The cackling mud hen built a veritable moat around Village Hall, save four seats in the entryway, "as the result of the continuous misinformation portrayed by the media and internet bloggers who are using Dolton as means to generate ratings and revenue" and threats of violence.

Being locked out, Dan Lee said, was an "insult to every single taxpayer in this city."

"This is a deflection from what's really happened in the village, all the money, what happened in Vegas," Thelma Gant added.

Trustee Kiana Belcher said: "To limit the access for everyday business that has to be taken care of, it's a problem. This is our tax dollars."

The community's residents could imbibe in the Supermayor's platitudes and promises, most certainly generated by a more lucid ghost writer, at the Thorntown Township website.

The Honorable Tiffany A. Henyard

"A successful business owner, community organizer, and director at large of the National Black Caucus Local Elected Officials, Tiffany A. Henyard began her public service in 2013 when she was elected as a Dolton trustee, and then mayor of Dolton in 2021. Henyard received the Chicago Anti-Eviction Campaign/Human Rights Defender Award, Chicago Honors "Community Activist of the Year Award," the Dorothy Brown & New Millenium of Women for Change—Government Commitment Award, and the prestigious "Queens Award" for Service to Community during the Covid-19 Crisis.

Under the leadership of Supervisor Henyard and the board of trustees, Thornton Township was awarded the 2022 Government Finance Organization of the US and Canada Award for financial reporting management, and transparency.

Supervisor Tiffany A. Henyard represents 158,000 residents across 17 municipalities and unincorporated areas. As the chief executive officer of Thornton Township, she serves as the chair of the township's board of trustees, manages the General assistance program and the township's department heads employees, programs, and day-to-day operations. Her statutory duties also include serving as treasurer for both the General Assistance and Road and Bridge funds.

Supervisor Henyard is a visionary leader spearheading the transformation of Thornton Township. Leveraging her experience as a community organizer, and entrepreneur, she has formulated a comprehensive agenda to remake township government.

Economic development stands at the forefront of Henyard's objectives. She envisions fostering economic development by establishing the Jobs Posting Board on the township website, and job training initiatives to connect employers and qualified job seekers. Through this initiative, she aims to cultivate sustainable employment opportunities to empower residents.

Education and youth empowerment also hold significant importance to Henyard's vision. Recognizing the crucial role of education, she strives to expand access to after-school tutoring, mentoring, and counseling initiatives which she sees as key components of her strategy to enhance opportunities for youth.

Community health and wellness are paramount concerns for Henyard. She is committed to improving the overall well-being of Thorntown Township residents. Her goals include increasing access to general assistance, affordable healthcare services, mental health resources, and promotion of healthy lifestyles. Henyard also addresses health disparities that disproportionately affect marginalized communities.

Social equality and justice are integral to Henyard's leadership approach. She advocates for an inclusive and fair society within Thornton Township, combatting systemic discrimination, reducing poverty, and bridging gaps in resource access to promoting social justice.

Collaboration and engagement are central to Henyard's strategy for change. She actively seeks input from residents through town hall meetings, Township talk forums, educational events, and community events to hear from youth, seniors, and families as stakeholders."

For individuals visiting the website as her dictatorship evolved, the message hurled many red flags, among them the awards for fiscal transparency and management, the treasurer guiding funds, resource access in the spirit of social justice, healthy lifestyles from someone so wayward, successful business owner and entrepreneur, encouraging citizen input, and the program for youth shepherded by sullen boyfriend Kamal Woods.

According to Cooking With Frank, Henyard was motivated to hone her entrepreneurial talent by a college instructor whose name she forgot. "Did she challenge you to make a scammin' ass hamburger joint that's based off a movie name? Do you honestly think Mark Cuban never heard of Good Burger? He's seen the movie."

Sheriff Frank runs Henyard's unpersuasive video promoting Tiffany's Good Burger and Soul Food, saying she not only intended to ballyhoo the restaurant on Shark Tank, but asked the billionaire for a $100,000 loan.

The commercial spells culinary "culunary," and features smartly decked-out Stanley Brown consuming a shredded, loosely hanging, pitiful sandwich with no discernible ground beef.

As the camera zooms in, Brown says "Now, you know that's not fair to sneak up on a man when he's eatin' a Tiffany juicy burger."

Cooking With Frank cooks Brown: "You should be ashamed of your African-ass self for doing this. Look at that nasty-ass shit. That don't even look like a hamburger. It looks like garbage."

He adds that Henyard probably never met the other two "nigger" actors in the ad before: "She found them outside on the bus stop smokin' a Newport with Leotis (Woods)."

A notice from South Suburban College expressed trepidation about cleanliness at the eatery:

"Good Burger has failed to steam, clean, sanitize or wipe specific equipment as required and the Café remains inadequately clean. Good Burger has failed to post, display, or provide Cook County Department of Public Health Sanitation reports."

The Supermayor treated constituents to her cuisine on the "Cooking With Tiff" You tube program, the name for which Frank says he did not take personally. "She act like we didn't see the Good Burger video. She act like we didn't see her squirt that jelly-like shit in the hamburgers with the same syringe."

An upset stomach from watching the video is not Frank's lone malady: "This woman is so ignorant it makes my head hurt."

Ignorance flourished at a small rally for the Supermayor inducing media attention. "Cigarette Break" Kamal Woods and Trustee Andrew Holmes, who voted incessantly with Henyard but was vocally dormant since the sexual assault allegations, had not lost their appetite as race merchants for belittling other black people.

"Some of y'all over there recording are black. Remember that. Remember you black. Never forget you're black," Woods warned grimly in his casual, thuggish white and blue jacket and ball cap. "You don't know how it feel to get beat down 365 days a year. You gonna keep chasin' here."

The "master class" in identity politics, according to Hannibal Is Hungry, persists with Holmes's meltdown:

"Watch how they (podcasters and other platforms) run with (this story). They put somethin' on social media. It is not only white folks are doin' it. We got the elite African American niggers who are doin' it. I watch You tube and I see what you guys are doin' out there for a dollar and the things you are doin' for a dollar. You need to get on your knees and work 'cause that's not how you make money."

Holmes said "they (the media and the establishment) did that with Martin. They did that with Malcolm. They tried Farrakhan. All of them failed." The trustee exhilarated that Dr. King "walked many miles and many streets not only in the state of Illinois and the county of Cook, but all across the United States."

Suddenly, it seemed through the shaming uncorked by Holmes, that Supermayor Tiffany A. Henyard was breathing the same rarified air as the biggest cultural and historical icon for African Americans.

The anguished, verbose Holmes preached racial solidarity:

"(Social media) send a message faster than you can tell the damn truth. Social media destroy friends, destroy brothers, destroy sisters, destroy families who tryin' to take care of their children. Social media is the gun that points at you. What is the use of doin' black history in school learnin' about how to advance? They (blacks) tryin' to destroy each other now. Check out social media with the new news, black on black crime."

"This is not the 1960's and Henyard is not marching in Washington," Hannibal Is Hungry advises as he ingests the derelict diatribe. "I know Henyard thinks she is the next Martin Luther King, Jr. I don't think a lot of people agree with that. It is a transparent attempt to shift the conversation from accountability to victimhood," calling it "the same tactic that Al Sharpton and a lot of these activists like to talk about. This is sidestepping--that is why a lot of people are tired of the Democratic party."

Holmes's chance for personal accountability happened when the assistant fired by the Supermayor, Fenia Dukes, openly discussed the Las Vegas trip.

Dukes once considered Henyard a caring person: "She took me under her wing. It was like mentoring. It was like learning different opportunities. She would say 'I'm teaching you the game, I want to teach you the opportunities I have because I am the first black woman mayor of Dolton. You could be takin' my seat.'"

Supermayor Henyard made her part of the entourage for a conference in Las Vegas that coincided with Dukes's birthday.

The evening of the assault perpetrated by Holmes, she said, they went out alone because their colleagues were otherwise committed. "I deemed him Uncle Drew. The mayor called him Uncle Drew. I've even been in places (with him) by myself plenty of times, even in cars, and he never gave me an inkling to harm me or make a pass. I legitly thought, you know, that I was gonna make it home until my last memory was me wakin' up in his room."

Dukes planned to establish the "We're Stronger Together," a foundation comforting and inspiring sexual assault victims. "I'm a survivor. I was done wrong. I'm fighting not just for me (but for other women)," Dukes said. "If nobody stands up for you, you have to stand up for you. We are survivors and we are gonna live again."

Holmes, an anti-gun violence crusader in Chicago, was fired by the Chicago Survivors organization he worked for: "Our mission is to provide crime victim services to family members of homicide victims, so our relationships with those families and our community is paramount. Without compromise, there needs to be an assumed high level of safety for the adults and children we serve."

An esteemed psychologist, Dr. Todd Grande, examined Henyard's lunacy as she luxuriated herself and her goons while the internet erupted concerning the fate of Dolton and Thornton Township.

"She has her own website where she refers to herself as the Supermayor. She also used this title in social media posts. She wrote about how there was much fanfare at her swearing-in ceremony (attended by dignitaries from across the state of Illinois). Tiffany mentioned how she was the first black supervisor of Thornton Township. She wrote how this sent shockwaves across the state of Illinois."

Her ascent, Dr. Grande posited, ballooned an ego spawning personal social media celebrations "which can be described as grandiose, attention-seeking, tacky, creepy, and demonstrating a profound lack of insight." His evaluation inferred that Tiffany A. Henyard is practically incapable of modifying, let alone recognizing, the consequences of her derangement.

"For example, she indicated that God chose her; she referred to herself as God's favorite. On Instagram she declared that she was the most powerful woman in the Southland of Chicago. In one post, she was featured with a dog wearing jewelry. The expression on the dog's face appears to communicate 'how was this woman elected mayor?'"

Ingratiated by God's blessing as she received a community service award, Dr. Grande quoted Henyard surpassing mere mortals in the annals of achievement: "I am Martin Luther King. I am Rosa Parks. I am Harriet Tubman. Y'all say Martin Luther King had a dream. I am the dream."

Dr. Grande derived a bevy of adjectives from his repertoire for the Supermayor: vindictive, bold, self-centered, arrogant, fearless, irresponsible, and entitled.

Henyard's election and appointment signaled a royal transformation, Dr. Grande contended, meaning everything should bear her magnificence. "I wouldn't be surprised if she thought about printing money with her picture on it."

Grande said she fancied herself the undisputed despot of the kingdom, ruling with an iron fist, crushing the opposition, syphoning and manipulating community treasure, and executing a spate of chicanery to retain power, including "trying to make black members on the board feel guilty about betraying another black person."

Dubbing her "comically incompetent," Dr. Grande alluded to her empty conscience: "She has no idea how others perceive her," and could probably care less.

Henyard's escapades and crimes, according to Dr. Grande, highlight the unfortunate susceptibility of smaller communities to con artists and schemers even though the people who endorsed her are culpable.

"How can the system be so broken that somebody like this is seemingly unstoppable?" he queried in abject disbelief.

CHAPTER V: CLOSING IN

In April of 2024, a "Take our Township Back" rally was held in the Village of Calumet City. Mary Avent, a retired Chicago police officer and member of the Thornton Township advisory committee to the trustees, joined nearly a hundred residents, including Trustee Chris Gonzales and Assessor Cassandra Elston, to demand greater government transparency and dismantle the leadership of Supervisor Henyard.

Avent, known for the expression "unass that seat" pillorying Henyard and destined to become a township trustee one year later, encouraged attendees to solicit help from local mayors, representatives, and other officials in the quest for change.

"It's sad to see what has happened," former Dolton Trustee Robert Pierson said. "The township did have a lot of benefits that it offered to residents. And now it's all gone. It's all about parties and bingo and putting your friends in positions that they don't know how to do."

"Every resident is a piece to the puzzle," Thelma Price said. "That is why our movement is successful."

By July, Henyard and her sketchy associates had alienated a coalition of Dolton trustees, including early ally Jason House who announced his candidacy for the next mayoral election and once confessed the Supermayor took him and colleagues "hook, line, and sinker" at the outset.

"We have to change the narrative around Dolton, and that begins today," House exclaimed. "We're going to have balanced budgets, and those balanced budgets will account for all of the mismanagement we've seen over the last years. No more first-class trips. No more security detail. We're going to save this town $1 million a year with one fatal swoop."

"Clean House 2025" was a play on words, mirroring those of the village clerk, Alison Key: "We need a clean house in 2025, not a hen yard."

"We've been locked out. We've been lied to," Trustee Kiana Belcher added. "We've been stolen from as a community from the current mayor and administration, and this must stop."

House doubled down: "Together with my colleagues on the board, we have been steadfast in our efforts to stop the gross mismanagement and abuse of power that people have seen in the village. We have a winning team. We will be restoring order, decency and dignity to this community."

House, a two-term trustee nattily attired in Joseph A. Bank sport coats and suits, severely contrasted the bellicose, ungrammatical mayor and her malignant goons. The University of Illinois-Champaign graduate is Illinois Healthcare Consortium chief financial officer, touted for banking and chamber of commerce experience.

The Supermayor baited House: "Just 'cause you wear a suit don't make you suitable."

Henyard's hyperbole was endless:

"Everybody wanna earn, but you don't want to learn."

"Don't hate, appreciate."

"You gotta give respect in order to get it."

"The world know who I am. Thank you, I appreciate it."

"At the end of the day they talk about Jesus Christ, so why do I think y'all not gonna do me the same way?"

Just Doing Nails revisits House's interaction with Henyard when they were both trustees, sharing a meeting video: "They had a kind of friendly relationship. I don't even know if I could say friendly, maybe acquaintance," she chuckles as House is seen embracing others. "You can see (Tiffany) 'hey what about me?' when he's coming in there. I don't think he wanted to give her a hug. Body language says a lot, alright."

She recalls a mentorship program announced by Trustee Henyard: "Please don't let this woman mentor your youth. She is not mentor material."

In the realm of politics making strange bedfellows, House was a member of Tiff-Tiff's "Dream Team" when she ran for mayor. Now, says Just Doing Nails, "He is the best candidate for mayor. He challenged her on the bills. Definitely, Tiffany has to go."

"If you're a subscriber, hit that Like button, and if you're new here hit that Like button too."

Portions of House's clashes with the Supermayor follow on the podcast.

95

Pertaining to vendors not being paid for work fulfilled, House says: "Checks were printed by the finance department, checks were presented to myself and the clerk (Alison Key), and we would sign the checks assuming they were approved on the warrant list. Once the checks were signed, they were handed back to the finance department. So, what happened beyond that point was beyond our knowledge."

The mayor bristles when House implies there was wrongdoing or sloppy accounting. "That's not a true statement," she chirps, arguing that checks he received to sign were for contracts the trustees voted to approve. "For the record, this body, this board, have voted to sign the checks but you refused to sign the checks," a decision House sometimes made knowing there were probably insufficient funds to cover them. "You're making up things. Stop."

Misuse of credit cards by the Henyard administration also incites Trustee House: "I didn't take any trips. I didn't fly anywhere. I didn't do anything else that benefited Jason House or anything improper. Any charge was done by the cardholder. All we're asking for is the documentation and the truth. So, whoever authorized that, it's their responsibility."

House alleges that emails, copied to the mayor, legal counsel, and the administrator wondering why some village employees were not being paid went unacknowledged. Detecting the dearth of transparency, trustees often said they were unable to execute decisions on proposals without requisite information about them prior to meetings.

"I have questions; questions are never answered. I've sent several emails," Belcher told Henyard in a meeting to discuss a village matter. "You've told your staff and everybody else not to answer our emails. We don't have an attorney we can trust to get valid answers."

Former Henyard chief of staff Dr. Nakita Cloud said, "She has never since she's been mayor responded herself to an email. Ever."

"We have no finance reports that have been given in the last seven months," House huffs. "And then they (Henyard and her flacks) talk about where the money is. We're gonna see another cloud of smoke and some other digital deflection."

Listeners imbibe:

"DAMN AMERICA IS GLAD THAT DOLTON IS ALMOST DONE WITH LIL WAYNE"

"Tiffany is another one who has embarrassed us"

"Hilarious hearing Tiffany complaining about paying bills when she can't even pay her rent."

"This woman is a sociopath, she is very dangerous. I hope the authorities investigate her illegal actions and put her away for a long long time"

"She always telling someone to learn, she appears to be good at scheming, and we all know people with demonic skills are Pathological Liars…"

"Trailer park Tiff, from Holland Nederland"

"Why does the mayor and some of her people say Mont instead of Month? Did they not take English classes in school? I think Tiff Tiff skipped school a lot. It hurts my ears listening to her."

From every indication, the Supermayor shrugged off emails throughout her tenure. "With something not being done, you can call my phone. As you guys know, I have a ton of meetings. What I'm aksin' movin' forward, if you have a problem, call my phone so we don't have to sit here at a board meeting and go back and forth."

House reiterates that he prefers email for the sake of documentation, and then accelerates his animus toward Henyard for suffocating trustee and citizen comments:

"The board meetings should be conducted with Robert's Rules of Order. If nobody else can talk, then why are we up here? There's no decency. There's no order. We so get the dictatorship that's being imposed here. We had about 15 residents that came up here (to speak). I didn't know any of them. All of them said do not let this be the worst administration you've ever seen. Then you turn around and give an hour and a half of (meaningless) dialogue and we're gonna have another one after this."

Just Doing Nails projects Henyard's angry concession to House's prediction with a graphic in capital letters:

"GOT THAT RIGHT!"

The host is praised for her platform:

"Great video I just can't believe this lady, she is all about herself and the people that are in her little circle. Karma is coming for her."

"Your content on this woman is outstanding!!! I'm from Baltimore but if I could I would love to participate in 'Clean House 2025' because Henyard has to go."

"I appreciate your soothing voice and commentary. Some You Tubers interrupt too much & and can be overly dramatic and too loud. Thank you."

House says that residents frequently ask him how he remains calm amid Henyard's bombast. Looking at the Supermayor, he says: "My response to all the clapback, all the videos she does, you just need to grow up. Represent this village with dignity. Please!"

Her viewers extoll him:

"Proud of you Mr House"

"Oh I love this man! He is so classy! He is very respectful when he has every reason not to be. Sir you give me hope."

Just Doing Nails simultaneously displays several trustees reacting to the bloviating Supermayor, including Kiana Belcher smiling like a Cheshire cat and shaking her head incredulously.

At one point, House looks over his shoulder at William Moore, a Henyard insider and charlatan reverend.: "Don't pray for me no more!"

Affirmation from cyberspace:

"'Don't pray for me no mo' that's when you know someone is pissed."

"That last part when he said 'don't pray for me no more was cold as hell'"

"Wow. 'William, don't pray for me no more' is so very damning… thank you for your digging and exposing the darkness."

Henyard relied upon the elderly to reverse her ebbing popularity with bingo nights, free food, and gratuitous grass cutting. In defense mode, she assails House for balking at projects that potentially lacked financing: "Are you not gonna allow the seniors that's on hold right now to get their windows and roofs completed before the weather breaks, trustee?"

Sporadic clapping emerges from the rear of the venue.

"So, what are you upset about, trustee? Can't give no answers."

A Just Doing Nails fan says:

"I want to see the list of people who REALLY got their ruffs (roofs) done and widas (windows) done"

House answers there are "$2.9 million reasons," alluding to unpaid vendors and other indiscretions. "Anybody who speaks that fast, watch your wallet!"

"Trustee! Trustee! Trustee! This why the meeting is getting outta order. Y'all expect respect to be respect," the Supermayor goads illiterately with muddled alliteration.

Illinois Comptroller Susan Mendoza suspended "offset" funding allocations to the Village of Dolton because "The mayor's office has refused to communicate with us or address the problem. If Mayor Henyard refuses to follow State law, my office will use the tools at our disposal to safeguard the interests of Dolton's citizens."

On the surface, especially for people unfamiliar with Supermayor Tiffany Henyard, Dr. Grande's comment about manufacturing dollar bills exhibiting her likeness might sound absurd. Since the inception of her tyranny, however, Thornton Township and the Village of Dolton weathered a Henyard tsunami entailing magazines, brochures, framed photographs in government buildings and elsewhere, posters, billboards, banners and memorabilia invariably overshadowing less relevant participants and details for initiatives and special events. Residents and other motorists traversing "her" communities assuredly gawked in amazement at the Supermayor's royal radiance beaming down from signs above the freeway:

TIFFANY A. HENYARD, KEEPING MY PROMISES

TIFFANY A. HENYARD, FIGHTING FOR MY RESIDENTS

TIFFANY A. HENYARD, THE PEOPLE'S CHOICE

HAPPY MARTIN LUTHER KING DAY 2024 (her photo was three times larger than the civil rights leader's)

She pulled out all the stops for Black History Month, sashaying in front of the Thornton Township building, verbally aligning herself with Martin Luther King, Jr., Harriet Tubman and Rosa Parks, guaranteeing a $1 million tax credit bonanza for residents, and repeatedly saying "Of course!" to emphasize her promises that AG Tactical considers an opportunistic travesty.

"She uses the media team at the township like her personal production team," Stephanie Wiedeman penned in a letter to the Lansing Journal. "Township residents pay these staff overtime for the movies she wants made for her social media and village board meeting presentations."

"It's Venezuela. Isn't that what they are doing out there with (President Nicolas) Maduro?" a 66-year-old resident asked. "His face is all over, like 'I'm a dictator.' There's no call for it. I've never seen a town more screwed up under her."

Podcaster Nate The Lawyer captures the scope of her mania, posting that he is "nothing special, just a guy and lawyer that likes to talk about the law. Let's look at the facts together. Let's also be clear these are my opinions alone. My mission is to make the law more accessible to everyone, whether or not you go to law school. Help me reach 1M subs."

Nate The Lawyer lists university police officer, assistant district attorney, law school lecturer, and director of the Law School Pipeline Program/Black Male endeavor as achievements.

"This this is the worst mayor in America," he says. "She makes sure that her face and likeness are paid to be put all over the Village of Dolton by the taxpayers," at a cost of at least $85,000, much of which has not been recouped by vendors.

He replays Trustee Jason House telling people why the braggadocio is so destructive:

"It is deeply unfortunate that this administration has chosen to squander funds on self-promotion while our fire department has gone without a contract for five years. This blatant disrespect is a slap in the face to the hardworking individuals and to the creditors burdened by the mayor's reckless spending."

This Nate The Lawyer episode displays bodycam video from a Dolton police officer responding to a complaint that banners in the village, mostly not paid for, were being removed.

With boyfriend Kamal Woods and Demarkus Criggley hovering in the shadows, Henyard confronts the Hispanic work crew, wondering "who told y'all to take them down?" as a bilingual female cop brokers the awkward moment and conversation.

The Supermayor claims that Administrator Keith Freeman, one of her illegal terminations, is the culprit. "Keith don't work for the village no mo. He's not the administrator, Michael Smith is."

Smith and another bogus hire, Police Chief Ronald Burge, Sr. also arrive at the scene as Henyard speaks of pressing charges against the Hispanics. According to a document provided by Nate The Lawyer, and drafted by the state's training and standards board, Burge, Sr. lacks law enforcement certification for not requalifying to possess a gun: "He is currently not authorized to exercise law enforcement authority or to carry a firearm publicly. We strongly encourage you to remove him from public service."

The Supermayor says the banners are "my property," a contrivance parroted by the officer to the laborers: "That's her property, so give it back," the officer demands while guaranteeing Henyard that a police report about the incident will be completed.

"I want all my signs. You got all my signs in the truck!" the Supermayor hollers. With that Criggley, linked to Henyard real estate transactions and possibly Airbnb's in conjunction with the Village of Dolton, is seen retrieving them from their vehicle.

An internet search revealed that Criggley, one of Henyard's mangy miscreants and a defendant in litigation and cases filed by the Illinois Public Risk Fund, managed Marks Express Investors and Criggley Elite Properties Enterprises: "My name is Demarkus Criggley. I am looking to connect with Buyers. Make sure to Friend me and Like my Connected Investor. I am a wholesaler out of Illinois with ton of properties"

Nate The Lawyer's viewers torch several elements of Henyard's audacious behavior:

"Her wanting to press charges against the workmen is a pretty good distillation of her character."

"Can she be arrested for murdering grammar on the English language?"

"That policewoman should be fired for the way she handled the situation!!! One it's not government property and two it's not your property till you pay for them. And this is a civil matter that should be handled in court. Using the police to oppress the people is a crime."

"Dolton is known worldwide as a place that is corrupt and doesn't pay their bills. Why should ANY vendor (like the banner printer) do business with the city?"

"Governor Jabba the Hut should resign for protecting her from prosecution."

"If you told someone about this, it's so insane no one would believe you."

"Police officers with long painted nails, and 'Supermayors'"

"The Chief of Police can't even be a deputy in Mayberry."

"This feels like it could be a comedy sketch, but here it is"

"When will this end? Gloom, despair, and agony on the residents of Dolton."

"How are we still talking about this criminal?"

Go Political host Carlton Flowers poses a contrasting question: "How could somebody be such a criminal genius? I know a lot of y'all think Mayor Henyard is stupid because she can't speak more than 4th grade English, even though she is Kooma Mo Latte."

Piped-in laughter ricochets the studio.

In the same vein, he wonders why an "idiot" manages to "operate in the dark underworld of Chicago."

"She's taking advantage of people with low IQ's," he theorizes, recalibrating the lies about lucrative incoming grants and her ungrammatical criticism that 'the trustees don't want to pay they bills.'"

"They get everything for FREEEEEEEEE," as banners "plaster your face and stupid sayings up and down Sibley Boulevard," Flowers says while recommending that "Stupormayor" Henyard place "booger" burgers on her political menu.

More laughter erupts.

Hannibal Is Hungry sums up the crisis in Thornton Township and the Village of Dolton: "Services are frozen, trustees are ghosting meetings, and residents are caught in the crossfire."

Even so, the "Friends of Tiffany Henyard Picnic" in September of 2024 cost Village of Dolton taxpayers $16,400 for equipment, personnel, food, and miscellaneous necessities.

The Supermayor was on the offensive: "Just like Trump, I'm gonna come in on a landslide."

Township resident Alicia Nichole bludgeoned Henyard at a meeting: "You're the biggest hypocrite I've ever seen in my life. One minute you're Team Kamala and the next minute you're Team Trump."

Indeed, Henyard sent the victorious Trump a fawning message:

"Congratulations President Trump!! You are now the 47th President. You have made history by coming back and winning the President of the United States. President Trump as the Supervisor of Thornton Township and Mayor of Dolton, I would like to sit down with you and talk about helping the people of Thornton Township. I have a lot of great ideas and believe we can work together for the greater good. With that being said let's Make America Great Again."

In December, the Lansing Journal printed a letter that Trustee Carmen Carlisle had emailed to Henyard without so much as a whisper in return. It appeared to be a good faith attempt at mutuality and productivity despite the growing volatility in the community.

"Dear Supervisor Henyard,

As Trustees of Thornton Township, we are dedicated to serving our residents and ensuring that our township functions in a way that reflects our shared commitment to excellence. To achieve this, we must work together in a respectful, professional, and cooperative manner.

We recognize that recent tensions have made it difficult to collaborate effectively. This has not only impacted the ability of the Board to work together but has also affected the community we serve. Reduced services and ongoing discord do not benefit anyone and are not reflective of the high standards our residents expect from their leaders.

We firmly believe that all stakeholders—Trustees, staff, and yourself —have an obligation to represent the Township with dignity and pride. There is a better way to govern, and we are ready to do our part to improve the situation. However, we also encourage you to take steps to avoid actions and decisions that might alienate the Board. Thoughtfulness in decision-making and a focus on community-centered agendas will go a long way toward restoring trust and progress.

To move forward, we respectfully request the following steps:

1. Professional conduct: Commit to fostering an environment of respect and professionalism in all interactions.

2. Open communication: Engage with us in a constructive and collaborative manner.

3. Collaborative agendas: Ensure the agendas reflect the collective agreement of all Board members, focusing on the needs of the community.

4. Trustee vacancy: Allow the members of the Township to vote for the vacant Trustee seat.

We are confident that, by working together on these points, we can overcome challenges and focus on the well-being of our residents. Let us also be clear that we cannot support any agenda that diverts from essential Township matters, such as bills, public comments, and critical services.

The decision to move forward is in your hands, and we trust that you will reflect on this letter thoughtfully. By prioritizing collaboration, professionalism and the community's needs, we can ensure that Thornton Township is represented with the care and respect it deserves. We remain hopeful and committed to finding a better path forward together."

Sincerely,

Trustee Carmen Carlisle,

On behalf of Trustee Chris Gonzalez.

Several developments, including the selection of Stephanie Wiedeman as a new trustee, were like dark, menacing storm clouds hanging over Henyard's hair hat.

Trustee Jerry Jones's absence constrained the Supermayor's power, creating a vacancy on the board that neutralized voting quorums when trustees did not attend meetings. A political game of cat and mouse resulted until Wiedeman, the executive assistant fired by Henyard as she assumed office, was picked to fill the void on an interim basis.

News For Reasonable People podcaster Sean Reynolds tells his audience that he was exercising on his treadmill at home when the live feed from South Holland, a Thornton Township village, recorded enormous applause as Wiedeman became trustee.

"You don't pour your life into 17 communities for somebody else to come in and watch it fall apart," Wiedeman said.

"People of the Township of Thornton, you deserve better, and for all of you Tiffany Henyard supporters, how's that working out for you?" Reynolds gloats. He admits, however, that she is probably too crafty, conceivably able to elude prosecution and incarceration, a "disappointing" opinion to his viewers disgusted by her unspeakable crimes and chicanery.

His site buttresses oral commentary and video clips with time stamped progression of the episode and a journalistically written synopsis:

00:00 Thornton Board Appoints Interim Trustee

02:00 Tiffany Henyard Skips Meeting, Setting Stage for Change

04:00 Controversy Surrounds Henyard's Appointment Power

06:00 Stephanie Wiedeman: A Return to Reason for Thornton Township

08:00 The Power Struggle: Chris Gonzalez and Stephanie Wiedeman's Strategy

10:00 Stephanie Wiedeman's Qualifications and Community Support

12:00 Tiffany Henyard's Leadership Under Fire

14:00 A Heated Election and Strong Community Response

16:00 The Future of Thornton Township: Budget and Insurance in Limbo

18:00 The Endgame: Henyard's Declining Influence and Upcoming Battles

20:00 A Critical View: Henyard's Ethical and Legal Challenges

According to News For Reasonable People:

"Thornton Township Supervisor Tiffany Henyard suffered a major blow as the court rejected her lawsuit, effectively limiting her key appointments before her term's end. Henyard, who skipped the meeting, faced resistance from trustees Chris Gonzalez and Carmen Carlisle, who strategically avoided meetings to block her attempts to install allies. Ultimately, Stephanie Wiedeman, a leader with over 10 years of experience, was appointed interim trustee amidst widespread support. The decision marks a turning point for the township addressing months of political gridlock that left public services stalled, including unpaid health insurance and halted bus operations. While Henyard's tenure has been mired in controversy and allegations of mismanagement, Wiedeman's appointment is seen as a step forward toward restoring accountability and functionality. This outcome signals a rejection of unchecked power and demand for political conservatism and community focused governance."

AG Tactical notices a sizeable chink in the Supermayor's armor as she continues to annihilate the English language. Not only that, the platform's mission statement, catering to firearms, mentions "Irrationality," and "Suspects," concurrent glimpses of the mayor's deteriorating mojo.

"Breaking Down Big Cases Where Suspects Act Irrationally! We attempt to learn from mistakes of the defendant and educate those who own guns for a safer country. I love to train and improve my knowledge while recording everything for your enjoyment and critique. I live in California so it will be fun to see how hard it is to obtain certain licenses (such as CLW). Come join the journey!"

AG's journey in this episode features biting wit.

The deputized podcaster peruses an online statement by the Supermayor riddled with embarrassing semantics.

"Why'd you go and irritate this lady? Y'all made Tiffany Henyard go full-on content creator. She's over here tellin' the truth." He pauses, then asks "What?" facetiously. "What?"

He worries about her mental health. "She did an hour-long live stream. She's losing her mind, folks. She's getting a little loopy. I thought she might have taken a few shots of Hennessey."

AG Tactical summons his audience: "Come along with me, man. I love you guys. We're at 42,000 subscribers, man, I'm on the road to 50. Everybody who just came in, Like that video, subscribe."

AG Tactical hears a grinning Tiff-Tiff do the same in the taped segment he is playing. "Hey guys, come on in! I love you too," she says to an admirer.

"She's trying a diplomatic approach. Let me seem like a normal person for a change," he says.

Henyard tries to jump-start her sputtering political jalopy: "This too shall pass. Just keep stayin' positive and lead with love. At the end of the day (one of her vacuous cliches), only you can fix it—you, you. Don't worry about the hate. Hopefully that's a little encourage for somebody this evening."

AG Tactical pounces on "encourage," an obvious derivative of encouragement. "The shit is horrendous, broh. This is a little like foreshadowing how fucked up this speech is gonna be."

Excoriating fakes news as incentive for the message, the Supermayor portends impossible brevity. "We gonna be here for a minute. I'll try not to be long-winded, I promise."

"It is my life's fucking duty to post the entire thing. I'm one of the fake news outlets," an annoyed AG Tactical says. "I'm going to stay up tonight and I'm going to watch this entire fucking video and make fun of you the entire day. You're not like any station on You tube. You're a fraud. All we see is a crazy lady with some shit glued to her head freakin' out about losin' her job."

The Supermayor, spitefully silencing people with unpleasant viewpoints over the years, urges township residents to attend meetings, magnanimously championing their participation in local governance "whether you want to vote yes or no, it's your choice."

Begins Henyard: "This is a statement regardings."

AG: "This is your mayor, Dolton. Please have somebody proofread it. Or are there too many morons on your team to proofread the letter?"

"The news is doing a smear campaign," rages the Supermayor between hyper gulps from her water bottle, "putting your community in jeopardy. My mom, my dad, my grandma, my family taught me get it from the horse's mouth."

"Your mouth is too fuckin' big. Close your mouth a little bit. Breathe through your nose," says AG, also begging her to stop using the hip hop phrase "lyin' on me" in the political arena.

Her lingual famine is flabbergasting:

"as critical ishills (issues)."

"workers' compazation (compensation)."

"ease central (essential)."

"underminding (undermining)."

"eggible (eligible)."

"hickstoric (historic)."

"It (hickstoric) sounds like a root," AG Tactical chuckles. "You want some of this hickstoric tea? Yeah, I was growin' it in my backyard. It cleanses your body."

He says the "knitpicking" would prolong his podcast by several hours because of the torrential errors. "Every other word is like an African prince trying to scam me."

AG Tactical trudges on through the morass. "You (the viewers) will probably have a stroke reading this," he regrets, displaying written visuals of the blunders. "It is bad for people prone to heart issues."

He finds her online presence puzzling. "You go to the meetings. Why don't you disprove the rumors over there? I hope this You tube is paying your rent."

Landlord Genetta Hall sought a special process server to deliver an eviction notice on a house being occupied by Henyard and Kamal "Leotis" Woods after months of unpaid rent. Hull, who leased to Henyard thinking they were cordial, said the "elusive" couple changed the locks on the doors, altered the garage code, and refused to vacate, meaning she could not, at the very least, inspect the premises.

"Do you know who these people are? Do you know who these defendants are?" the exasperated Hull asked the judge.

Social media posts savage the Supermayor's treachery:

"That awkward moment when you're such a shit person even the landlord looks sympathetic."

"Another rising star of the democratic machine."

"I don't understand why she is making over 300k a year and still renting instead of buying property."

"It's as if that one kid who always tried to cheat off your math homework to the point where you put wrong answers down when you knew she was looking, was elected mayor."

"Probably a big red flag when the person in charge of your city can't or won't pay their rent."

"Boots on the ground" investigative advocate Jedidah Hall and a cadre of comrades protested on the sidewalk across from Henyard's South Harvard Street digs while drinking coffee on a frigid winter night to stay warm.

"We want answers!"

"Rape is bad!"

"We don't like coverups."

"Hey-hey, ho-ho, Tiffany Henyard's got to go!"

A female voice is heard behind Jedidiah: "The people wanna know, the people in social media wanna know, the citizens of Dolton wanna know" whether the Supermayor plans to offer a scintilla of accountability for her actions and policies.

Henyard's father appears in the driveway.

"Are you okay with everything you hear? Is there any kind of response from the father of the mayor?" Brown asks.

Henyard's dad barely speaks, even when Brown tells him Loretta Hall's mother is present, wondering when they will get out of her daughter's home.

Woods emerges from the house next, sparking verbal ugliness with his nemesis Jedidiah.

"You know what we do to you," Woods says.

Jedidiah: "What's you doin' to me?"

Woods: "You know what time it is."

Their volatility escalates, with not all of Woods's smack talk being audible.

Jedidiah's verbiage, however, is clear:

"Don't play with me fool! Come over here dummy!"

"Come right here, come right here, nigger! You're a weak ass nigger!"

Jedidiah does not spare Demarkus Criggley, another one of Henyard's goons: "Take that fake tough ass home, nigger."

Eventually, both men enter the street with Woods the first to turn back around, preventing fisticuffs.

Jedidah badgers Kamal about hiding his expensive BMW allegedly purchased with taxpayers' money, and questions the impetus for seducing Henyard:

"You don't even love that girl. You don't even love her, nigger."

Tiff-tiff is now outside as well in her woolen hat, most likely guarding another wig from the elements.

"That's the mayor! That's a whole mayor! Do y'all see that?" observes a lady in Jedidah's group, sardonically conveying that the sighting engenders awe.

Police cruisers arrive and, according to the video recording, officers are not overtly confrontational with Brown and his cohorts. At first,

Jedidiah says, "Y'all still protectin' them. Why you not adressin' them? They agitatin' and it's on camera."

Then he mellows: "I don't even know these officers. I am not against y'all."

There were no arrests and, based on the circumstances surrounding the ruckus, a judge rejected Henyard's quest to obtain a restraining order against Jedidiah Brown.

In essence, The Supermayor and her boyfriend were deadbeat squatters, the bane of local government jurisdictions around the country.

Unconfirmed hearsay haunted cyberspace regarding a "Help Tiffany Henyard Save Dolton" GoFundMe page defraying debt from her legal battles, attacks by political antagonists, and endeavors to better the community.

In this episode, IamJ9eve relays the initial Dolton board meeting of 2025 amid various village and township government operations curtailing because of fiscal constraints and chaos.

"Hey momma. I made!! first time on a live"

"Hi from Victoria BC"

"Momma shoutout Houston, TX"

Rumors fly that Henyard might skip the meeting owing to a "credible threat" against her.

"Cooking With Frank says Tiff is afraid of some 'credible threat.' I don't know if Tiff sees herself as some mob boss and about being gunned down in a drive-by," a listener offers.

"Stan (Brown) is there."

"Hopefully 2025 is the year of accountability. Love the pink mic."

"hello funny girl you should be a comedian."

"What will Tiffany be wearing tonight?" What color? I'm predicting red," the host says.

Fashion suggestions surge among her followers:

"Leopard skin"

"Purple dress from Amazon"

"Hopefully she'll be wearing handcuffs and prison suit soon."

"She going to come out thugged-out pants sagging."

"We all know she's wearing a fishing wire, orange wig."

"Black and white stripes."

A chorus of meeting attendees are singing "We All Need Somebody to Lean On" by Bill Withers from the early 1970s.

Jedidiah is there, orchestrating a familiar chant: "Hey-hey, ho-ho, Tiffany has got to go."

More viewer insights:

"The truth of the matter is our votes must count. We got a township closed, we got a village hall closed, and now she want to call in a threat. She is the outright, unadulterated threat."

"Clearwater Beach, Florida, in the house."

"I will never respect someone who chose to fire a sexual assault victim to keep an alleged predator Andrew Holmes in a seat just to vote her way."

"Almost all special events she held were illegal without trustee approval. The skating rink is deplorable now."

"I would never respect nor vote for someone who close down business unless they agree to pay to play so that she and her boyfriend can ride around in style using our tax dollars."

"Dolton is aware and awake."

"Tiffany's goons trolling the HELL"

Henyard is a no-show.

Former Village of Dolton Trustee Valeria Stubbs asserts herself in the meeting:

"I'm askin' everybody to come out in droves February 25th, 2025 to clean house," Stubbs says before thumping Trustee Stanley Brown, a sniveling Henyard lackey. "Mr. Brown, I am so disappointed in you, I could throw up."

Angela Hubbard, the mother of Henyard's landlord, denigrates the AWOL Supermayor for not paying rent and being a scourge:

"I've been watchin' all your shenanigans for about four years. We will do our due diligence for future tenants—an example, maybe even fingerprints and blood drawn. I once heard you quote Dr. King about the dream. No, Tiffany, you are a nightmare."

IamJ9eve threads:

"What do you expect from criminals?"

"The Roast of Henyard."

"I stand with Jedidiah Brown a wise man who knows how to advocate truth and justice."

"Did you see Jarediah whatever his name is they were at the Supermayor's house and Tiffany's boyfriend came out talkin' smack and they're all standing out there Tiffany and her people smoking weed they called the police."

"She can be late, not show up; it will make no difference," unremitting resident Dan Lee says at the podium as the live stream delivers. "We're in a movement. We can do this—whether she likes it or not is irrelevant."

Lee's remarks spark podcast elation:

"I stood up and clapped from home."

"I made a homemade banana split to watch this. Banana, vanilla ice cream, black cherry jelly and crunchy peanut butter."

"What's up y'all?"

"Smash them likes."

"Hit that Subscribe."

"It's that time again."

"Cooking With Frank."

Frank, the de facto sheriff of the Podcaster Posse, happily launches this episode by saying that "to protect the sheep, you gotta catch a wolf, and it takes a wolf to catch a wolf."

The previous night at a hastily held Democratic caucus, State Senator Napoleon Harris won the nomination for the Thornton of Township Supervisor's election in April. A technicality helped torpedo Henyard, who arrived punctually for once, because an assessor was omitted from her slate. The Supermayor stood in the middle of the packed venue screaming "Illegal, Napoleon!" at Harris, who is also Thornton Township Democratic committeeman commanding the power to caucus. Henyard's lawyer sued, claiming the first caucus in 30 years was irregular and that a second one should be convened. Henyard said erroneously that 500 supporters were denied entry as they stood outside in the cold. Cook County Circuit Court Judge Caroline Moreland ruled that the deadline had passed for any objections to be valid.

"The big dog stepped on your ass last night, Henyard. You a pit bull in a skirt—what you did is you ran into a fuckin' werewolf," prods Frank, laughing at her henchmen for not confronting Harris, a handsome, imposing former 245-pound NFL linebacker for the Raiders, Vikings, and Chiefs. "Y'all niggers is cowards."

"It's a wrap! It's a wrap! She cannot run!" a videographer at the meeting is heard saying. Henyard, tail between her legs, bolts for the exit as relieved attendees sing "nah-nah-nah-nah, nah-nah-nah-nah, hey-hey, goodbye," a tune dispatching teams losing to the south side's Chicago White Sox through the years.

Cooking With Frank reports that Demarkus Criggley, one of the "mud waddling" hen's goons and the baby daddy of 11 children, rescued a box of T-shirts in defeat.

"Maybe she'll open another hood burger or something," Frank muses. "Y'all didn't look like the dominating force" that physically intimidated people in the past. He tells Kamal "Leotis" Woods that "all that $100,000 a year to do nothin' is over with, bruh."

Viewers land a few haymakers:

"She really wanted that seat she's been campaigning since day 1 with all of those give aways"

"Lost fair and square…everything was legal. Get over it!!!!!!!! Thanks COOKING WITH FRANK"

"Liar, liar hair on fire"

"They had to pack the hall to get the results they wanted…"

"let me find out your a local, Frank…lol regardless, thank you for your coverage and dedication!"

"Hair Hat Tubman, Martin Luther Leotis…Civil Wrongs Leaders of Dolton"

"There is footage of Tiffany in the building the entire time before the caucus. She lied that she didn't get in the building until after 6:30. She is on video tape that she was in there hours before. She is standing with Kamal, holding her child, and three other guys. She is standing on the other side where the cameras are not focused, however one content creator did capture her hours before."

"It's bad here in Chicago. I'm leaving within the next two months. I'm out."

"Damn Frank is cooking"

Cooking With Frank extends a "shoutout" to AG Tactical and Hannibal Is Hungry, proficient podcasters hunting the Supermayor.

A Just Doing Nails adherent theorizes why the Democratic Party of Illinois, an infamous flotilla of corrosive crookedness, put the clamps on Tiffany A. Henyard:

"Had she demonstrated more loyalty to the party they likely would not have taken so much drastic measures against her. Tiffany might have remained on the ballot had she simply stayed quiet and avoided praising the opposition (Donald Trump, whom she compared to her mythical political comeback). So, thank the good Lord for her big illiterate mouth Tiffany Henyard has no political prospects whatsoever. Let's be clear: they are not doing this out of concern for the residents. They feel betrayed by one of their own, so they are kicking their puppet out."

While there was euphoria, Henyard had announced her re-election bid for mayor in the Village of Dolton, colliding head-on with Trustee Jason House in the Democratic primary February 25. "It's time to be the change that is needed in the South land," she obstinately said.

Two of Henyard's flacks, Michael Smith and Keith Price, were among those uselessly petitioning that Napoleon Harris was ineligible to pursue the supervisor role on grounds he resided in Flossmoor, outside the township boundaries.

"I think enough people know her name to write her name in, and I believe we could still win it," Price said.

Sheriff Frank borrows a sports analogy from another podcaster:

"That's like a football game and you down 40 points and there's two minutes left in the fourth quarter and you out there tryin' to kick a field goal. The game is over. Take your punk ass to the locker room."

As for Henyard's lagging prowess:

"You were not qualified to be the mayor, and you were not qualified to be supervisor or the liquor commissioner, or Good Burger restaurant owner or any fucking thing. She is incapable of working with other people in any capacity," Frank says.

The crazed, hypocritical Supermayor angrily labeled the caucus "a hostile takeover. They were gonna cheat. And what I can't stand for is people bullying other people."

"The real business isn't being done because of all this nonsense," 33-year township resident Darrell Lathan said. "We need some action; somebody that's actually going to do their job, someone that's actually going to work for the people, not themselves and have pictures all over the place. We don't need that."

Recognizing the importance of community newspapers to constituents, Senator Harris issued a statement in the Lansing Journal.

"Dear Thornton Township Residents,

I want to take a moment to personally thank you for your continued support and participation in our Democratic Caucus held on December 3, 2024. It is because of your engagement and commitment to our community that we can ensure our collected voices are heard and our shared values are upheld.

As we embark on this new chapter, I want to assure you that under my administration, we remain steadfast in our dedication to Thornton Township. Our primary focus will be on delivering critical services, maintaining a balanced budget, practicing fiscal responsibility, and preserving the integrity and trustworthiness of Thornton Township.

I, like you, have witnessed the distractions and challenges that can sometimes arise. However, I am committed to ensuring that Thornton Township is a beacon of stability and progress. Together, we will move beyond the noise and focus on what truly matters—serving residents and making our community stronger, more vibrant, and more united.

As a resident and servant of this township, I promise to stand true to my values of Thornton Township. With your continued support, we will uphold the standards of excellence that our community deserves as we move forward into this political campaign season.

Thank you all for your faith in me and for standing with me as we work together to secure a brighter future for Thornton Township. God bless you, and God bless all the residents of our great township."

Best,

Napoleon B. Harris III

Thornton Township Democratic Committeeman

Attorney Max Solomon sued Harris and the Thornton Township Democrat Caucus on behalf of Henyard, tagging Village of Dixmoor Mayor Fitzgerald Roberts as co-plaintiff without his permission.

"My focus is on the Village of Dixmoor and helping the residents here," Roberts said. "I have no desire to be part of this lawsuit."

The Journal was a handy conduit for communication. Publisher Melanie Jongsma conducted "fact-checking" in the teeth of Henyard's "claims and accusations," saying "how important it is for this local newspaper to have created a record of meetings that have taken place. We have published videos and articles of Thornton Township meetings throughout Tiffany Henyard's tenure as supervisor, so we are able to look back and look at them."

Meanwhile, social advocate Jedidiah Brown hailed the efforts of the Podcaster Posse to resolutely hound and demolish Henyard and her hoodlums:

"I try my best to tell people what's goin' on. (Henyard) knows the day is getting closer. We know she feels the pressure. I'm asking for everybody out there, because y'all are the best detectives, get the information and share as much as you can because it's effective, it's working, and together I guarantee you we're gonna take down this corrupt administration."

CHAPTER VI: THE SHOOTOUT

Tiffany A. Henyard was destined to go down swinging—literally. In a rare appearance at the first township meeting for new Trustee Stephanie Wiedeman in late January of 2025, the Supermayor was irate that the board voted to place employees Kamal Woods and William Moore on paid leave pending forensic audits of their job performance. Pouring salt in her highness's wound was the fact that Wiedeman made the motion.

"This is political retaliation," the Supermayor claimed as she disparaged Wiedeman's level of education, "because y'all just pickin' on certain individuals. Y'all didn't come here and do no research."

Hannibal Is Hungry compliments video of the meeting with annotations provided by the Lansing Journal that, enduring the Henyard debacle, boosted its You tube presence while interfacing with podcasters. "I like how they put things together."

"No! No! No!"

"Your minutes are up."

"She can't read."

Attendees, emboldened by intermittent hoots, shouts, and laughter, dread the Soooooooopermayor's pompous pontificating.

She thanks them for their diminishing support even though her ship is sinking faster than the Titanic, and the stock market in 1929, barely projecting above the commotion. "Don't be like the bitter people you see or just got so much negativity. Find peace in everything you do. I will succeed in everything I do. I want you to know that I love you—there's nothing you can do about that. Keep God first, stay prayered up."

One of her tireless naysayers, Dan Lee, mercifully initiates public sentiments following the sermon: "We have to go through this endless filibuster at the end of meetings. I'd like to suggest to the trustees that they move the supervisor's report so that those of us who don't want to listen to the blabber can leave."

A viewer weighs in:

"As soon as Dan Lee starts talking, Tiffany Henyard starts coloring her Denny's placemat."

"She never gives the residents respect, yet she wants everyone to respect her in that seat," Vivian Allen says with Henyard doodling and dropping her head apathetically. "You might wanna just step down and not come to another meeting."

"This whole thing that's been happening here has been awful. The world is watching us; the country is watching us; the state of Illinois and the communities are watching us," Beth McBride asserts. "I want to say to the world that I am so appreciative for the many prayers around the world. I've read many comments on blogs that are praying for us. I've also read they are encouraging us."

Cheers accompany the speakers.

"By April you will be out of both seats," Jennifer Robertz forecasts, attracting more applause.

Mentioning Henyard's bullies, Alicia Nichole says "how monumental this day is for me because William (Moore) you're out of here," as the bearded Moore gazes impassively.

Janell Taylor, a well-dressed elderly woman wearing a hearing aid, tests the microphone wondering whether it has been sabotaged by Moore or some other Henyard toady:

"At the last meeting, we had a young lady who got up here, and who had not even signed up to speak, and she used a lot of profanity and there were two children in the audience. Our Supermayor was smiling like it was cute, and she did not have her head down as she has it down now. I don't understand, if you're a woman lift your head up and listen to what's said, whether you accept it or not."

Taylor levels Darlene Gray Everett, the suppressed trustee donning a Covid mask, with unwavering loyalty to the Supermayor: "Why do you have to sidebar with the Supermayor during these meetings? Couldn't she call you on the phone and tell you how to vote?"

Henyard attempts to cut her off.

"Aw, shut up girl. My time isn't up."

It wasn't the first Henyard rodeo for Taylor, who reminds Cooking With Frank of his grandmother. In the past, she had mentioned a "rogue vehicle," the BMW driven by Kamal Woods, reportedly on the public dole, reciting the analogy "where there's smoke, there's fire." She finished by saying: "I'd like a BMW myself. Can I have one?"

Finally, Jedidiah Brown lowers the boom on Tiff-Tiff about her unverifiable college education and other deficiencies as laughter, histrionics, and clapping permeate the room: "You got questionable spendin' habits, you got a failed business venture—your restaurant was deemed nasty," precisely the way he portrays her as a person. "(Stephanie Wiedeman) didn't fuck her way to the top. You'll never be a married woman. I had four or five people tell me how they had to take care of (your child)."

"You gone, bitch."

Brown departs the lectern, walking towards his seat near the front while Kamal "Leotis" Woods and Demarkus Criggley stand at the back of the venue. Something is said that prompts Brown to reverse field, moving in the direction of the two men he has verbally sparred with before.

It turns physical as Jedidiah and Woods tumble to the floor and nearly a dozen people converge, including the Supermayor who maneuvers the table and sprints headlong into the melee, losing a shoe and dislodging her hair hat. Although they do not look capable of puncturing a wet paper bag, let alone erasing the legend of Bruce Lee, Criggley kicks Jedidiah several times when he is down. Lavelle Redmond, one of Henyard's controversial, momentary hires and supposedly another former boyfriend, is seen cocking his fist, throwing a couple of rapier right hands, and siding with Brown in the donnybrook.

"It looks like (Henyard's) striking," Hannibal says. "She's in the fight. A man is getting jumped and she's gonna jump in."

Mortified residents flee the premises. An unidentified onlooker hastily surveys the scene, saying: "Y'all women go out. He kicked a man while he was on the ground. That ain't right. What kinda goon he is."

Trustee Chris Gonzalez and Henyard sycophant William Moore exchanged finger pointing and words as the dust settled.

"I have never seen a politician jump in and fight like that," attendee Meghan Dudek said. "It was scary and horrible—it is an embarrassment."

Hannibal Is Hungry believes security should have detected and mitigated the looming hostilities.

Podcast audience members agree:

"(Security) had his hands in his pocket. he was a waste of space!!! he did not to get control on the situation. he should be fired!!!!"

"LET'S GET READY TO RUMBLE!"

"Definitely a (Henyard) farewell speech. She knew the fight was gonna go down. Quigley was looking at Leotis for signals the whole time Jed was speaking."

"Are we really surprised? Is there something in the water in Illinois? We talk about scandalous mayors—Tiffany Henyard in number one—but there are others," admits Hannibal Is Hungry while pondering why no one was arrested.

Perusing video clips, Cooking With Frank notices that "Weasel" Moore enters the fray, along with viewers taunting the combatants:

"Kamal and Criggley don't have any kind of hands."

"Damn, Leotis got some chicken legs."

"Did her wig stand up by itself, when it fell off, cause you know she hasn't cleaned that wig since she got it."

AG Tactical says Henyard overrated Woods's ability to frighten enemies: "Well, guess what Tiffany? There's a lot more harder people than Kamal, your burned-out, smokey-smelling boyfriend."

Demarkus Criggley was later arrested without incident for stealing Lavelle Redmond's phone in the altercation.

Lansing Journal Publisher Melanie Jongsma blamed Jedidiah Brown in a statement she made on You tube, saying the brawl was "instigated by someone who doesn't live here, someone whose goal was to provoke a reaction and create a sensation. He succeeded."

Her opinion incurred fervent backlash from viewers and newspaper subscribers:

"Disappointed in the Lansing Journal. Anyone who watched this from the beginning saw the business as usual by the supervisor. This appeared to be a set up."

"Did anyone notice the two men in black that got up and stood in the aisle right before Jed started talking? They knew he was coming up and planned to attack him"

"Either way, Tiffany left a space of safety to become a combatant in a fight her married boyfriend started"

"I can't believe the opening of this video placing blame on a person who is a resident and didn't mention once that the supervisor, leader of the board, took off her shoes, moved the table, ran into an active fight, and began assaulting people unnecessarily."

"I'm so disappointed that you called the last person speaking an instigator. He was speaking what I feel most people are feeling about Henyard. Her idiot boyfriend had no business saying anything to Jed. I hope Jed presses charges."

"Jed did not start this fight nor did he swing first. He has been stalked and harassed by tiffs goons and married boyfriend. An apology needs to be issued or we will start a petition against this platform. I'm unsubscribing."

"This is Thornton Township under Tiffany Henyard's leadership. An entire CLOWN SHOW! You owe Jed and the township an apology."

"Does anyone else who isn't a resident, feel completely involved in this? It truly hurts my heart."

"This is the legacy of Tiffany Henyard"

Part of the legacy, Jedidiah Brown clarified, was the expletive he unloaded on the Supermayor: "They've historically called me a bitch first. We basically greet each other with that word now. Each one have called me a bitch. Tiffany has called me a bitch, Criggley has called me a bitch, and Kamal has called me a bitch."

Brown said, "I waited 'til I was struck and then I responded."

Even though the brawl transpired at the township, Henyard invented a conspiracy theory implicating the village board: "I have been attacked, stalked by individuals that have been hired by Trustee Kiana Belcher, Trustee Jason House, Trustee Tammie Brown, and Trustee Brittney Norwood; all hired these individuals to come into our town and create chaos, individuals that have so much hate that they are willing to put me, my daughter, my family in harm's way."

Thornton Township trustees Stephanie Wiedeman, Carmen Carlisle, and Chris Gonzalez detached themselves from the frenzy, publicly saying they were "deeply disturbed by the events that transpired during last night's board meeting. As public officials, we are entrusted with leading through professionalism, integrity, and respect. What began as a productive discussion on critical community matters descended into chaos and violence, behavior that has no place in Thornton Township and will not be tolerated."

According to Actual Justice Warrior Sean Fitzgerald, Henyard's demented persona is appealing for several reasons, calling her "one of our absolute favorites on this channel, somebody who has definitely paid for many meals and a huge portion of my wedding due to you guys loving Supermayor content."

Guilty pleasure from his audience:

"I see Supermayor…I click!"

"The Supermayor died for our sins"

Trying not to get "wigged out," Nate The Lawyer and his viewers indulge:

"When you (Nate) said little bigwig. I lost it"

"I need the pics of supermayor without her blonde wig…please release them!"

"Township residents MOPPED UP THE FLOOR WITH TIFF'S WIG"

"When wigs fly"

The wig-worn Supermayor and legal counsel Beau "Brisket" Brindley cast aspersions on her colleagues and alleged she protected Jamal because Jedidiah was wielding a knife, something that the video stream revealed as a microphone.

Playing the sociopathic victim, Henyard and her lawyers sued an incalculable number of people for defamation, character assassination, false "allezayshuns," sabotaging the system, and other cruelty.

"Do everybody know what their employees (referencing the conduct of Woods and others) do? I understand everybody want me to be the target," she blustered in a pathetic attempt at speaking English. "I understand they want me to be the bad guy for everything that goes on in the village but that's not the truth."

Actual Justice Warrior listeners are skeptical:

"How is she innocent? Video evidence of assaulting people was broadcast across the nation."

"It was something I expected from a Boondocks episode or Don't Be a Menace….."

"Her tenure as a politician should be called 'New Jack City. Part 2.'"

"Not crimes, just 'allezayshuns' against a beautiful blatt woman."

"A mayor speaking ghetto"

You tubers at the Lansing Journal channel denounced Darlene Gray Everett's complicity in Henyard's hideousness:

"Trustee Darlene Gray is every bit as much to blame here as Tiffany Henyard, in that Gray Everett has completely neglected her responsibility as a trustee to help put an end to all this. The community should never forget what Gray Everett has done and hold her accountable."

"Anyone else notice that Tiffany Henyard said a couple of times the vote would be "two against two"? How would she KNOW Gray Everett (or Evers as she calls her) would ALWAYS vote WITH her if she wasn't controlling her?"

Donkor Parker, who was tossed to the curb by Henyard, also challenged the reticent Gray Everett aggressively at a meeting.

Excerpts from a lengthy Chicago Tribune editorial were sobering for the community:

"You gone, b----.

Those harsh words spoken at a podium by a critic of Tiffany Henyard during a Jan. 28 Thornton Township board meeting preceded a brawl. Video shows Henyard joined in the melee. Security reportedly had to clear the room after fighting intensified. It was a shocking display at a government meeting, and that's a high bar these days, but it's no surprise tempers are high in Dolton, where Henyard serves as Thornton Township supervisor as well as mayor of the village. She makes a good living from her government roles, earning a total of $270,000 annually.

Her role as supervisor is the primary contributor, earning her $224,000 a year. If she's ousted, an ordinance the township board of trustees approved in 2023 will see her successor earn just $25,000.

Voters have a chance to put an end to the madness in a matter of weeks, when they vote to elect the next mayor, who will hopefully prioritize showing up at meetings, something Henyard doesn't always do. Henyard's been tossed off the ballot in Thornton Township, and now her last hope to remain in power rests upon the Dolton mayoral outcome.

There's good reason to want change, if only to provide some sense of stability. Henyard's name has become synonymous with controversy, including financial mismanagement, corruption and misuse of power. What this means for the citizens of Dolton is chaos and uncertainty. In Dolton, residents can't even be sure their garbage will be collected.

Henyard is under investigation for various business and financial records related to her administration. One of her key allies, Deputy police Chief Lewis Lacey, was charged in federal court with bankruptcy fraud, making false statements and declarations in a bankruptcy case, and perjury in August. Henyard's administration has been marred by so much scandal that 56% of Dolton voters elected to recall her in 2022, though a judge ruled the votes could not be certified.

The editorial board wants to see the south suburbs prosper. That can't happen if suburban leaders engage in public scuffles with their political critics. Voters in both Dolton and Thornton Township have a chance for a fresh start—they should take it."

Sean Reynolds of News For Reasonable People is on the same page: "If you re-elect Tiffany Henyard, that's on you. I don't want to see the citizens of Dolton played with, toyed with, having their village meetings just a spectacle, the township meetings a spectacle, for worldwide media. It's nuts."

"If you have checked out some of Tiffany Henyard's biggest supporters on Facebook, they have deleted their profiles and deleted their posts about Tiffany Henyard," Hannibal Is Hungry points out while blasting two-time gubernatorial candidate Tio Hardiman, the executive director of Violence Interrupters. "Maybe you finally realize that she is in trouble and finally realize this is not just a joke, that this is not just an attack on a single black woman in power, but this is a corrupt person that has f----- up the entire town of Dolton and f----- up the township."

Documentarian Tommy G returned to Dolton as Henyard's fiefdom faltered. The grinning Supermayor was superficially friendly emerging from her office. Tommy G produced the lease for the Tahoes with her signature that she said was forged. "Cigarette Break" Kamal Woods uttered "BAM-BAM-BAM," strongly implicating finance manager Robert Hunt, not his girlfriend, in the monetary mayhem roiling the community while Keith Price looked on morosely and deceptively denied knowing Henyard adversary Dr. Nicole Scott of the FREE-N-DEED grocery outlet.

Asked to describe the Supermayor in the piece, Valeria Stubbs said: "Only one word come to mind—demon—possessed."

"She takes people and gives them the most they ever made," was Dr. Nakita Cloud's explanation for why any rational person would support Henyard.

Tommy G encountered street urchins hired by Henyard to bolster interest in her campaign, one of whom threatened to get physical before backing down.

A video, perceived as desperately unflattering, surfaced of the Supermayor and "Keithopotamus" Price pulling up to a cash-checking store.

IamJ9eve's listeners are clicking on all cylinders:

"Whoever got this footage was nosey at the right time"

"She switched wigs to change her identity but the walk is still the same."

"She needs money to get a new WIG to replace the one she lost in the BRAWL."

"A city check made out to her. She cashing it out all she can before prison"

"She is picking up Lee-Otis Newports. Because he can't come outside"

"Anytime a MAYOR/SUPERVISOR walks into a check cashing place means the beginning of the end…..she will be the first mayor/supervisor in HISTORY to be caught walking into a check cashing place….soooooo hood"

"Ohh how the mighty have fallen. She went from hopping out of bulletproof Tahoe's with a security team. To hopping out regular with Keith Price as security"

"Keith Price stepped out of that van like Diabetes is going to catch up with him before he gets arrested."

"Look at this man tryin' to get out that car—this is a cargo van—that shit is effort for him," Cooking With Frank says. "Now you see why he didn't throw any blows. Now you see why he's all talk. He'll look at you mean and bark at you, but his ass ain't gonna do anything physical."

With the opaque FBI investigation, Cooking With Frank tells the audience that "all they have to do is watch You tube (Podcaster Posse deputies Hannibal Is Hungry, AG Tactical, Jedidiah Brown, and a few others). You got more than enough shit to throw Tiffany Henyard away for a long time. A person with a loud-ass mouth like Tiffany Henyard—they can't shut up—all you got to do is listen and they will tell on themselves."

"The 'Hoodrat Chronicles', presented by your host, none other than Frank…bon appetit!" a satisfied follower says.

A few days after the brawl, more than 300 residents and officials participated in a Zoom call requesting that Governor J.R. Pritzker, Attorney General Kwame Raoul, and Cook County State's Attorney Eileen O'Neill Burke oust the Supermayor from office.

"So, I plead today alongside everybody involved, that the governor and the state's attorney give the people what they already said they wanted," Jedidah Brown said, "and that was for them to step up and remove this so it doesn't go on another day."

The next township board meeting witnessed heightened police presence. The Supermayor was missing, obviously the major reason for the jovial mood.

An imaginary chorus of munchkins were heard from the rafters:

Ding, dong!

The Witch is dead.

Which old Witch?

The Wicked Witch.

Ding, dong!

The Wicked Witch is dead.

Wake up, you sleepy head.

Rub your eyes, get out of bed.

Wake up, the Wicked Witch is dead.

She's gone where the goblins go—

below, below, below.

Yo-ho, let's open up and

sing and ring the bells out.

Ding, dong!

The merry-ho,

sing it high, sing it low.

Let them know

the Wicked Witch is dead.

When life insurance policies for Village of Dolton employees were cancelled over non-payment and government buildings closed temporarily, Jedidiah Brown organized a march to Pritzker's Chicago home. "While they're posturing on national issues against Trump, are they doing anything about local issues under their roof? They gotta act. The governor can't keep kicking the can down the road."

The protest proved to be mostly symbolic, as no contact materialized with the governor. Cyberspace, though, was rife with a political hailstorm:

"Remember when Pritzker endorsed her? He was so proud. Now he looks like he never heard of her."

"hell the Democrats would vote her into president."

"Queen Mayor Tiffany Cuntavious Ghetto Fabulous. She most likely gives him a regular mouth massage to stay in office."

"Sorry people, that was a waste of time. The fat gluttonous slob of a pigman Governor PiGster is more corrupt than she is."

"Pritzker only worried about keeping J-6 MAGA Republicans from state jobs. If you're a Democrat politician and steal from your voters you're not a crook it's your God given right."

"dummycrats put this HYENA in office."

"What has the Democrat governor of Illinois done to assist the residents of Dolton and Thornton Township, of removing a corrupt Mayor/Supervisor Tiffany Henyard? The Democrat party is corrupt, and they rather protect illegal aliens, with the taxpayers money."

"Without attempting to sound politically incorrect, especially with the political climate in Illinois, why is the Illinois States Attorney and the governor attempting to protect people illegally in the country? But they are silent on protecting the legal residents of TT and Dolton in exercising their constitutional individual rights to address their government?"

That week, the Department of Justice (DOJ) sued the State of Illinois, the City of Chicago, and Cook County for their unconstitutional sanctuaries "intended effort to obstruct the Federal government's enforcement of federal immigration law to impede consultation and communication between federal, state, and local law enforcement officials that is necessary for federal officials to carry out federal immigration law and keep Americans safe."

CHAPTER VII: THE CAPTURE

Convening a special township meeting, trustees Wiedeman, Gonzalez, and Carlisle voted to terminate Henyard vermin William "Weasel" Moore, listed as executive assistant, and youth intervention director Kamal "Leotis" Woods. The Supermayor, her board (bored) sycophant Darlene Gray Everett, and Clerk Loretta Wells did not attend.

Usually seen distributing water bottles and information packets at meetings, Moore was Henyard's maestro of microphones adjusted and functioning sporadically to fit her narrative. Lansing Journal Managing Editor Carole Sharwarko said Moore, a "divisive character," also often loudly berated attendees brave enough to contradict the Supermayor.

"The technical issues surrounding the mics at the meetings is a running joke because Tiffany's always works crystal clear, but when anyone else needs to talk like the trustees and the residents all of a sudden they have technical problems with everyone else's mic," Just Doing Nails notes. "It's done on purpose. It is a literal silencing of the people's voices."

Most residents found Reverend Moore, also known as "The Vampire of Village Hall," repugnant for alternating religious conviction and bully tactics at meetings. Laughter, hoots, hollers, and "no-no-no-no" infiltrated one of his last prayers as a government employee, erasing any semblance of credibility:

"Precious father, we thank you for the spirit we have in this particular place, Lord; in every heart and every mind. Thank you right now, Father, in leading this government as you've instructed it. We understand that not all men have faith. Father, we trust you, we believe you, we love you—we give you glory; we give you honor; we give you praise. Continue to give our leaders a heart of courage, passion, and compassion for our people. In Jesus' name, Amen."

Religious zeal and "compassionate" appeals did not dissuade trustees on an ordained crusade to vanquish Henyard's nasty ruffians. "I feel like at least one of them was the perpetrator of the violence," said Gonzalez, presiding pro tempore in Henyard's absence. "And (Moore) was being very disrespectful to residents."

Wiedeman added: "As a township employee, as any government employee who is paid with taxpayers' funds, I think that we are expected to be held to a different standard. That comes with different levels of respect."

Viewers at podcaster AK COLE'S perch welcome the news:

"$200,000 saved today. Way to go tuff tiff."

"I knew they were placing them on paid leave for this reason. The stupid mayor is going down in flames and there ain't nuttin she can do 'bout it…"

"BEAUTIFUL. PROFESSIONAL. EXPEDITIOUS."

"It's a great day today…The dominos are falling one by one."

"Too bad they couldn't make a motion to fire Tiff"

"Kamal will no doubt go back to his wife! Because the money is drying out."

"Kamal is surely hoodwinked and bamboozled now, shaking his head, a victim of politrix."

"This just in. Thornton Township trustees also approved a motion to transfer food pantry security guard Keith Price to his new role as Thornton Parade Float."

With the countdown to the Democratic mayoral Village of Dolton primary pitting Henyard and Jason House only two weeks away, IamJ9eve warns against complacency:

"It's very important to remind people not thinking someone can win something because in your world, your bubble, everybody hates her. It's not true," IamJ9eve says, noting that she may have been gullible without knowing the entire sordid history of the Supermayor.

The podcaster plays video of Henyard, the self-puffing champion of disenfranchised underdogs, handing out food boxes to people driving nice cars, and attacking her foes: "I've been doing this since I've been in office. I haven't stopped and I won't stop. That's the difference between me and them."

Feedback from viewers is mixed as they brace for more mischief:

"There's no way in the world that she'll get reelected."

"The crazy thing she has a lot of people on her side that ride or die for her"

"She needs to lose and get the boot out of office"

"You're gonna show up and vote to make this happen."

"I bet she gets re-elected."

AG Tactical remembers the meager 9.5% voter turnout when Henyard triumphed initially, saying there should be far more participation this year: "There's one good thing that Tiffany did—she got everyone in Dolton aware—for a nice amount of years, I see people in Dolton a lot more aware of what's going on with the electoral situation because of Tiffany."

He speaks of "Tiffany A. Henyard: The People's Mayor," saying "I'm gonna miss the whole slogan; I'm gonna miss the energy; I'm gonna miss the cocaine," as she and Demarkus Criggley are seen on another silly snow removal escapade.

Leading up to the election, Henyard was interviewed on Chicago radio station WVON by Cleopatra Draper, fielding "softball" questions as she did previously while speaking to slovenly race huckstering slob Roland Martin and the Way Up talk host. Hardly immaculate, Draper was caught stealing her opponent's signs in a political campaign.

Just Doing Nails reviles the Supermayor for crowning herself another Rosa Parks:

"I tell everybody I am her, I am Rosa Parks," Henyard regales Draper. "The difference between back then and now is I'm livin' the same dream as her. What did she not want to do? Give up her seat, right? What I'm doin' today? Not givin' up my seat!"

The assertion is "blasphemy" and "despicable" from a "race baiting" woman, Just Doing Nails says. "You are the mayor and the supervisor. You have privilege in these seats. Quit usin' (race) as a shield."

In other words, Henyard's enormous seat, the throne hijacking approximately $300,000 a year from the taxpayers, and Rosa's digs on the bus were not even remotely equivalent.

"Draper act like she's Teflon Tahoe Tiffany lawyer by telling her she don't have to answer the question! What a freaking joke. I guess it takes a thief to know a thief," a Just Doing Nails listener quips.

"Kleptopatra" Draper, a Cooking With Frank designation, enjoys Henyard's stories, one of which alleged that she snared $300 to $400 a day peddling snacks in high school, that go over like a concrete kite on the internet:

"300 Dollars selling cupcakes!!! What else was in them, or was the cup solid gold? Is there no end to this woman's claims to fame?"

"I just be realized that if Henyard's mouth is moving then she's lying. I realize that her imbecility is off the charts but she can't even make her own lies somewhat believable."

"Does she think it's because the coke has kicked in, and she gets all animated, and moving her hands, and looking like that blowfish (Sheriff) Frank was referring to that we believe her? She is not trying to convince nobody but herself."

Turning off the township spending spigot, Stephanie Wiedeman, Chris Gonzalez and Carmen Carlisle voted unanimously against budgeting $36,000 worth of special events, including Spring Fling, Fiesta, Country & Western Shindig, and two for Valentine's Day. In addition, they rejected Henyard's phony 100% tax refund for residents.

Barking at breakneck speed on the heels of dodging another meeting, the double-dipping Henyard used Facebook to rally Village of Dolton mayoral constituents in the eleventh hour from her township office, spurring the attention of Illinois Leaks, a watchdog group reciting the State Officials and Employees Ethics Act:

"At no time shall any executive or legislative branch constitutional officer or any official, director, supervisor or State employee intentionally misappropriate the services of any State employee requiring that State employee to perform any prohibited political action (i) as part of that employee's State duties, (ii) as a condition of State employment, or (iii) during any time off that is compensated by the State (such as vacation, personal or compensatory time off)."

"She decides to go on these long rants with the same old, same old spiel," Hannibal Is Hungry reckons.

"Please do research before you vote 'cause a lot of people got a lot of misinformation," she says, repeating fears about knives at meetings and the "chaos agents" orchestrated by trustees Wiedeman, Gonzalez, and "Carliar" Carlisle. "I want to go home to my baby. Period."

After erroneously promising to produce receipts negating her fiscal malfeasance and saying mayoral foe Jason House has been committing bank fraud and writing illegal checks, she begs residents to "stay woke," stop impugning their own race, and exile the social media herd seeking "clicks and views to make off drama."

Most galling, perhaps, is the racial cheap shot she takes at local law enforcement, once her bodyguards and companions. "My complexion don't match my protection."

"I love you and there's nothin' you can do about it!"

Hannibal Is Hungry viewers never cease to be amazed:

"Supermayor ran and jumped into the middle of a fight between two grown men and other people, probably wasn't thinking about her 5 year old daughter, but is afraid to sit in a town meeting."

"Portrait of somebody becoming unhinged"

"Holy COKE-a-cola I thought she was on 3x speed."

"RESIGN!!!!!!!! Nobody cares what you think!!!!!!!!"

"When your toilet needs repair and won't stop gurgling, you have the same noise that comes out of this super-sap. Does she ever STFU?"

"Now we know where the other half of the eight ball went"

"All else fails yell about how black you are and how unfair it is. What does that have to do with stealing money?"

The lax financials were coming home to roost for Dolton. State Bank notified the village that $76,138 was owed on 13 leased vehicles, six of them police patrol cruisers, with payments having been defaulted since May of 2023. The bank threatened to repossess them.

Interest in Henyard, "a ghetto mess" and a "hot ratchet mess" with national and global ramifications is evidenced when podcaster Chawanne Burns greets listeners from Texas, Baltimore, Michigan, San Diego, and Germany watching the Facebook fallacies perpetrated from Town Hall while the meeting was being held.

"It's always got to do with racism and sexism when things don't go her way," remarks Burns, who is not buying the knife allegation and argues Henyard remains at fault in the brawl with her orange wig resembling a "tangerine" or an "orangutan" flying around.

The hoopla among her tribe is hilarious:

"Do do brown mouth."

"She would make a good birdie in a life-size coo-coo clock."

"democrats and Roland fartin can't save u now"

Burns regurgitates some of Henyard's most outrageous lies, urging people "not to forget who you are dealing with."

"Here we are at the end of this story," Nate The Lawyer says nostalgically while Henyard is ditching the meeting. "I do a lot of public corruption stories, right? The one thing I get from a lot of people not in the United States (he mentions Ghana and South Africa, for instance) is I didn't know the United States could have crazy politicians like we do here."

His listeners are wistful:

"Here we go again. no golden mic means no Tiff"

"Damn! And I went and made popcorn all for nothing."

"What? I'm ready for the next season. If we give Thornton Township money you think they'd hire her back?"

"When Tiffany is gone what are we going to talk about?"

"It's been a journey hasn't it"

"It's getting close to the end, Nate. I'm going to miss you and others' great coverage of the Supermayor"

News For Reasonable People candidly admits selfish reasons for wanting Henyard to stick around: "I would love nothing more if she got elected because I'd have podcasts for years, years!"

Indeed, Henyard was the embarrassingly magnetic magistrate of uncivil decorum, hubris, and avarice in governance. But the winds were out of her sails; she was treading water with the possibility of drowning.

The advent of the undeniably influential Podcaster Posse intersected with so-called legacy, traditional "mainstream" media throughout the Tiffany Henyard holocaust, a product of the internet and cyberspace in this rapidly changing technological world.

Lansing Journal Publisher Melanie Jongsma and Managing Editor Carole Sharwarko were initially refused admission, despite press credentials, to a township meeting without Tiffany Henyard in mid-February for not being "mainstream" media mostly entailing Chicago network television stations. With residents imbibing virtually in another room because of "security" concerns, gelatinous Supermayor henchman Keith Price roamed the building, unable to eject vigilant anti-Henyard streamers Vivian Allen and Alicia Nichole from the chambers.

In the months of confusion and collusion, Price was Henyard's jack-of-all-trades administrator, food pantry chump, spokesman, and enforcer. The former Village of Harvey alderman, school board member, and park district commissioner also owed the State of Illinois $37,000 in unpaid filing fees for a political action committee. As alderman, he broke the jaw of a mechanic who was parking vehicles illegally.

Trustee Chris Gonzalez was stonewalled by Henyard when he asked about the ubiquitous Price:

"What is Mr. Price's title, and was he board-approved for that title?"

Henyard: "You already know his title."

"No, I do not."

Henyard: "I'm not gonna play that."

The scenario with Price, the Lansing Journal, and community advocates fueled online conjecture about Henyard's administration and how media are defined in contemporary America:

"The situation had Tiffany written all over it. Glad they weren't intimidated. Just another ploy."

"I believe citizen journalists are an important part of the story and should continue their efforts. I disagree with Tiffany's team trying to silence them."

"Don't worry things will soon change once Tiff and her goons are gone."

"I believe that whether you're part of a big corporate media outlet, local news like the Lansing Journal, or an independent Youtuber we're all in the same game—we just serve different masters"

"Having a press pass is earned. It means you are acknowledged as main stream media."

"Lansing Journal presents the most balanced coverage. The 'big' channels want big dramatic sound bites that don't necessarily represent the scope of the activities of the meetings."

"As YouTubers, we're uncensored, shining a light on the things everyday citizens don't usually get to see."

"I became aware of what was going on from YouTube Content Creators coverage."

"The Constitution is our press pass."

One week from the mayoral election and with early voting underway, Just Doing Nails shares the latest Facebook foray of Henyard, attired in pink pajamas and winter coat, strolling near campaign signs in adjoining yards.

"I'm here to calm your fear," assures Just Doing Nails in her patented eloquence. "Tiffany Henyard has made an art of grifting and making it as though she's someone she's not. So, this little campaign display is no exception. So, while she's standing in front of multiple signs in a row, the signs are in the same vicinity of her parents' house."

Her viewers smell a retrofitted rat:

"The signs are photoshopped, you can see they don't have legs in the grass, which by the way is frozen solid right now because it's below 32."

"Great detective work! Did those signs look photoshopped to you? They were kind of floating, lol."

"Another fantastic video! She is getting slaughtered with early voting. She has not even been out at the polls. I am being conservative when I say it's 8 to 1 in favor of Team Clean House"

"Let us hope and pray she never finds any employment in the public sector after Feb 25."

Several neighbors said Henyard planted signs in their yards, but they had no intention of voting for her. Snake-in-the-grass Demarkus Criggley, meanwhile, was observed stealing Jason House signs.

Buoyed by #TrustGod, #blackhistory, #istandwithtiff, #leadwithlove, #nevergiveup, and #iwasmadeforthis hashtags, the strident Supermayor does not relent:

"Thank you residents for your love and continued support Thank you for the calls, text messages and emails We look forward to our next chapter of rebuilding the village. I'm excited for Unity"

"We wouldn't have to rebuild it if you didn't tear it down," Just Doing Nails says.

Nonetheless, the Supermayor is a social media oddity and sensation:

"Can't wait for the movie. Who plays Henyard?"

"The Jerry Springer Southside Traveling Road Show"

"She looks like E.T. when they dressed him up as an old lady."

"Hopefully this won't hurt Henyard's chances to be the Democratic nominee for President in 2028."

Her Facebook faithful won't surrender:

"Tiffany's going to win. She's the incumbent. The opposing slate has no chance."

"Praying you win the election there's no one else cares like you even if I'm not from Dolton I see the good you do for those that do live there."

"You should run for the Governor of Illinois. I'll vote for you."

Cooking With Frank says that Henyard's prediction of a landslide matching Donald Trump's is preposterous. "I heard you already gettin' your ass kicked in the Dolton mayor race. Someone close to the situation, they say it is like 9 to 1. You'll be on the opposite end of the landslide. The landslide will be rolling your punk ass over. You'll be under the landslide."

Humorously hopeful responses resonate:

"She kills me talking about winning by a landslide not gonna happen it be more like a mudslide for real."

"Henyard is about as good as a burnt grilled cheese sandwich"

"2/25/25—let's hope they get it done finally. And she can take her old school broom colored wig on somewhere."

Jedidiah Brown and Lavelle Redmond filed federal lawsuits against Henyard and her henchmen alleging that the donnybrook at the Village of South Holland township meeting constituted "retaliation for exercising" the rights to free speech, expression and association. The litigation specified that Redmond attempted to "mediate and prevent any physical altercation" before Kamal Woods attacked amid lackadaisical police protection. It also named two private security guards accused of detaining and pummeling Jedidiah in a separate room.

Earlier accusations by the Supermayor manifested in a lawsuit alleging that Dolton elected officials, Thornton Township trustees, and public relations guru Nakita Cloud hired Jedidiah Brown to agitate and harass Henyard and Kamal "Leotis" Woods for months leading up to the fracas.

"(Brown's) language was strictly intended to incite Mr. Woods to react to the verbal attacks against his significant other," it stated.

"It's an outrageous claim," Dolton mayoral candidate Jason House said. "It's a waste of oxygen."

"Just lots of allegations, not much behind them. Just more baseless stuff," opined township Trustee Chris Gonzalez, who no doubt continued to regret his nomination of the hellbent Henyard for supervisor.

In likely an act of drug-addled dementia afflicting the Henyard camp's litigious lunacy, Thornton Township was also sued for $10 million on behalf of "Cigarette Break" Woods for emotional distress and wrongful termination.

Cooking With Frank calculates the payout at $100,000 a month over a decade to someone who never spoke "even one time, answering a single question regarding what he actually does, not producing one child that can say 'Leotis helped me out.'"

Substance abuse is suspected:

"It's the Audacity for me, Leotis really believe his lawsuit has any merit. What goes on in these people's minds, the township needs to sue him for their money back."

"The Newport car, outfit, and Denzel 'where da rocks' at hilarious!!!"

"I've always said both of them are on cocaine. That's why they don't have no money. Say no to drugs."

"The new Bobby and Whitney...they definitely got to be on that good stuff.."

Their bravado was fading; the walls were closing in on the Supermayor's renegade reign.

AG Tactical shows Henyard in an empty parking lot saying she is "lovin' on the people."

"The only people I see are her boyfriend and some random man trying to plug his business," the podcaster muses. "I don't want Tiffany Henyard lovin' on me without my consent. I feel violated."

Wannabe rapper Tiffany A. Henyard burdened constituents with "I'm feedin' the people, they put me in office and treat me like it's illegal to feed the people" in a skit reputedly photographed several days prior to the election by Unk low down, the Village of Dolton public works superintendent parodied by Cooking With Frank.

"Nobody in their right mind would put out a terrible ass rap song," Frank says. "She look like the rest of the hood rat broads that be tryin' to rap—got on their little hair hats, little microphones and shit break dancin', whatever the fuck they be doin'."

Frank's flock feast on the farce:

"She went from Temu 'Soo-pah Maya" to Temu rapper. This is comedy gold!"

"It's Lil Wayne in a Weave!"

"She needs a straight jacket"

"Oh shit! If that rap was a prize fight, somebody would have stopped it!"

"All I could think when I saw this was WHISKEY TANGO FOXTROT?"

"One thing about narcissists…no matter how many people think they are slow, they see themselves as the best thing in the world…all self-esteem and zero self-awareness"

"She's done."

"I'm ridin' from Vegas to Chicago in Tahoe's," Henyard raps tauntingly at her rivals with an image of Malcolm X in the background.

"She's going to be petty. She's not giving an inch," Hannibal Is Hungry says about the woman who helped swell his subscribers over 100,000.

The prodigious posse member refers to local government as a "blood sport," teeming with "personal vendettas. It becomes a play. You have a community where everyone knows each other."

AK COLE excavates a Henyard campaign caper containing clips of Jedidiah Brown charging the stage at a Trump rally and contemplating suicide along Lake Shore Drive in Chicago.

"I hesitated to share this video, but I believe it needs to be addressed. The content she posted is inappropriate and concerning. Mentioning a suicide attempt is simply unacceptable. While sharing her video won't necessarily improve the situation, it's important for people to see how far she is willing to go and the depths to which she will sink."

A listener echoes his contention:

"This is sick and twisted. She dropped this on the anniversary of Jedidiah's emotional breakdown."

The sun is setting on the Henyard charade, according to Nate The Lawyer's brethren:

"Last night I was driving South out of Chicago and was greeted by a massive billboard of Tiffany Henyard and another off the side of I-94 south. It was hilarious. Lock her azz up"

"I am tuning into this circus weekly from the UK. These clowns be clowning everyone. I hope the community get back what is theirs and get rid of these clearly corrupt snakes."

"It should be personal, very personal against the person who used two entire towns as her personal fiefdom and made the townsfolk pay for her luxuries while most of them are living in poverty."

"She reminds me of those dictators that won't stop till the people force them to flee the country."

With Henyard vilifier Dan Lee manning the phones as an extra and visuals of well-coiffed candidates comporting themselves in a refreshingly dignified manner, the ad designed to hamstring Henyard's regime impressed:

"This election is about progress, about real leadership that puts the people first. With Alison Key for village clerk, Edward Steave, Kiana Belcher and Brittney Norwood for trustees, we have the leadership to move Dolton forward. Dolton deserves leadership that you can trust. Make your voice heard. Vote Jason House for mayor and Clean House 2025."

An internet insider enthuses:

"Lord I can't WAIT for election night!! The Crash Out is gonna be EPIC!!"

The Lansing Journal received a cogent, cathartic post:

"The people no longer want to entertain the court jesters who have made a mockery of the entire township and Southland. The brave and powerful voices of the citizens have been loud and clear. To borrow a quote from a failed national democratic campaign, it is time to 'turn the page' on Henyard et al. It is also time to end the chapter and close the entire book."

The receipts from Henyard's spending sprees were never retrieved or publicized. "She's playin' a game," Cooking With Frank ascertains. "She knows damn well she doesn't have the receipts that we're looking for. It's either that or her stupid ass don't know what the fuck a receipt is."

The weekend preceding the election, his listeners realize they are on the home stretch:

"Tiff is proof that the Twilight Zone really exists"

"When will Snow Black and the 7 dumb dumbs go away"

"When Tiffany loses she will claim they rigged the machines demand a recount."

"Will Dalton have a parade when Tiff is voted out?"

"Tuesday is the big day when Tiffany loses the Democrats primary to Jason House."

With the posse closing in, Henyard hurled grenades from her foxhole hideout alleging property tax hikes by the trustees, rejected grants that she procured, violation of statutes called "statues," a bogus Lightfoot investigation, kickback collusion, the virtues of Stanley Brown, the arrest of Jason House by the FBI that was disproven, and a false story about a fire truck being stolen by a unionized Dolton firefighter who supported Jason House.

"There's only one person on the board that has a mugshot," House tells Nate The Lawyer.

"I can see the move backfiring," Hannibal Is Hungry says the night before the election. "The firefighters are among the most respected public servants. They ain't the cops. That's why there isn't any song that says 'f--- the firefighters.'"

"Salute to y'all! One more day for Hentard to get voted out in a landslide victory by Clean House 2025! She will be mayor until May so the cookin' will continue...until she is locked up," Frank promises.

On the morning of the election, the Supermayor was singing her new rap chart buster "Feed the People" at the Lester Long Fieldhouse voting precinct and spouting off:

"I see no competition so when I come in with a landslide this evening, it's gonna be so great—y'all can come to the after party and we can talk about it."

"I just recently saw a video of her rapping," Dolton resident Sharon Hunley regretted. "Like, that's just not a good look. You're in politics, you're supposed to be leading the people."

A group of House backers gathered at a grocery store on the main drag, Sibley Boulevard, imploring people to vote. The first few hours, voting was on pace to double or triple the last election.

Regan Lewis said Dolton had become "kinda like a joke" thanks to Henyard. "It's embarrassing."

"Everybody is just looking for change right now," said Thomas Shelton, who made the mistake of voting for Henyard in 2021. "So, I just came out to do my duty, to vote—just try and get that change."

Buyer's remorse also applied to Loretta Barnes as she voted at Diekman Elementary School: "She's been bad news, and I think we are in a real mess right now."

"I just think the town has really gone downhill; a lot of businesses have closed up," Benjamin Willis said.

Huffed Henyard: "I'm going to unite my community when I get rid of this board. They say clean house. They're damn right. We're going to clean house today, starting with the board of trustees. That's every last one of them, including the clerk."

House welcomed the challenge: "She's running from her responsibilities. I figure if you want to pass the buck with the trustees, you can pass the seat with it. We have seen four years of failure, and we cannot continue down this path. We want to make sure we can change the narrative and show people what this community is really made of."

"HELP US GET RID OF CORRUPTION" screamed from the Supermayor's social media platform trimmed in pink and white. Miserable minion William "Weasel" Moore traded barbs with Clean House 2025 supporters and handed pamphlets to voters entering a polling site.

Hannibal Is Hungry expects a deliriously ungracious Henyard in defeat:

"Monique Owens, the first black mayor of Eastpointe, Michigan, just delivered one of the most unhinged speeches in political history. After losing her re-election in a landslide and facing fraud charges, Owens compared herself to Martin Luther King Jr., Malcolm X, and even Jesus Christ. The speech is so delusional that it feels like a preview of how Tiffany Henyard will go out if she loses her election."

House swamped the Supermayor 3,896 votes to 536 in the Democratic primary, a whopping 88% testimonial.

AK COLE breaks the news with "Jason House Projected Winner! Tiffany Sent Packin'" as residents applaud the verdict, eliciting kudos:

"Congrats from New Jersey!"

"Congrats from Philly!!!"

"Now I can rest We Did It!"

"Well, she said it would be a landslide"

"Yes!! Congrats Jason!!!"

"Congratulations Dolton! I've been rooting for you all"

"Praise God!"

"I feel ecstatic. The voters have spoken. They've spoken in a loud way," House said with his trustee teammates and Clerk Alison Key riding the winning wave to a festive soiree. "I've said it before—and I will always say it—this does not represent Dolton. We had one rogue individual. Tonight is the new day for the community of Dolton."

"The Wicked Witch of the West is dead," said Lawrence Gardner, whose trucking and U-Haul enterprise was grounded by Henyard. "It's over. Now we have to go another eight weeks to bury her."

Less than eight weeks later, an inferno burned his business to the ground. "The fire is suspicious in nature," the Dolton deputy fire chief said. "We do have the fire marshal out here with our (mutual aid) arson team."

"OMG Mr. Larry the tow truck driver. He was the FIRST to speak out against Tuff Tiff. Hope he is insured," a Cooking With Frank viewer says.

Among the revelers for Team House was Stanley Brown, the crawling chameleon and Village of Dolton trustee whose detrimental allegiance to Tiffany A. Henyard should have precluded him from being there.

That afternoon, FBI agents hand-delivered subpoenas to Dolton Town Hall requesting records pertaining to St. Patrick's, the multi-story restaurant, bar and banquet business on property once owned by Kamal "Leotis" Woods. Inspections, violations, complaints, and ownership documentation were also sought through "all correspondence including emails, phone calls and text messages."

Proprietor Tiffany Kamara said Henyard and Woods "wanted to take our land," hence the reason for procedural delays and obstructed liquor licenses hoping to foreclose the endeavor.

"Trust the process. Watch my comeback…Stay tuned……wait y'all thought I was finish hell no," Henyard posted in ungrammatical defiance.

With the notorious Supermayor reduced to governmental obsolescence and fantasies, House faced independent Casundra Hopson-Jordan in the April general election.

"She got the stuffing beat out of her," said Valeria Stubbs, who battled Henyard toe-to-toe and garnered an at-large township seat. "If I can do a backwards flip right now—and I'm 67-years-old this month—I would definitely do it."

Cooking With Frank fans celebrate the outcome:

"Frank, WE DID IT! DOLTON RISING!"

"The BLOW runs out tonight!!!!"

"Ding Dong, the witch is dead!!"

"Congrats, Frank, on all the hard work and success. It has been a long fight for sure. May no one allow another Tiff to run their community again. Salute Frank!!!!"

For all intents and purposes, Henyard's goose was cooked by Frank and others planning her political demise. Tantrums, pernicious plots, and legal wrangling could not rescue her.

Napoleon Harris sprinted to victory in the race for Thornton Township supervisor with the Supermayor scrounging 193 write-in votes.

Feisty Trustee-elect Mary Avent, who blistered Henyard on numerous occasions, guaranteed vigilance to the new supervisor: "I'm one of those people, I ordered all the books on what the township is about, what each position is, and Napoleon I'm going to keep you to your word. I'm going to keep you in check. We're going to do what we're supposed to do."

The indignant Tiffany Aiesha Henyard ghosted meetings in the twilight of her atrocities and chicanery. Fledgling Mayor Jason House, after annihilating the acerbic Hopson-Jordan at the ballot box, and fellow trustees swiftly approved more than a dozen business licenses squelched by Henyard's woeful administration.

"We do have a long line of businesses that have been done wrong over the last four years, and that is stifling the growth of this city and this entire community," vigilant crusader Dan Lee insisted.

Trustee Kiana Belcher was emphatic: "Dolton united. That's our new movement. Dolton united! That's our new movement!"

Hannibal Is Hungry succinctly offers a requiem of Henyard's rampage amid a false rumor she had fled to Victorville, California, theories the Supermayor and Kamal were feuding, the new MAYOR Jason House sign adorning Village Hall, reports of intensifying FBI inquiries, supposition she was pregnant, and photos of the couple wandering around Atlanta.

"The serious part—the press wasn't watching this—not at first. The state didn't seem to care. But eventually the people had enough. The residents themselves stepped up and shined the light. They brought the chaos to social media. They brought the videos. They dropped receipts and showed the world how ridiculous it has gotten. What was once small-town drama turned to national headlines because regular people got fed up and started hitting record. And now Tiffany has lost it all—she is no longer the mayor; she is no longer township supervisor. The empire she built on intimidation and ego crumbled under the weight of truth."

Henyard's last food giveaway failed to hoodwink or bamboozle women waiting in the drive-through:

"I did not vote for that woman, but I'm gonna get me something to eat today," Dana Richardson said.

Gert Holleman made a pragmatic distinction, saying "I like the giveaways, but I don't like her. She is nasty."

"She's giving back what we already gave," Roslynn Phillips added prophetically as WGN's Ben Bradley revealed Henyard raided the public coffers in her final year of power for $347,680 entailing base salaries, expense allowances, and bonuses.

"It just proves that what she was doing was very selfish," Stephanie Wiedman concluded. "It wasn't about the people."

When Bradley approached her, Henyard was irritated:

"Why you out here?"

A social media soldier provides the answer:

"Because I love you, and there's nothing you can do about it."

While the proverbial "madder than a wet hen" could have prevailed at the event, her cocky strut conveyed zero humility, let alone recognition of the thorough repudiation delivered by the voters. She was levitating in a deranged, unsatiated, strangely nostalgic dream of subjugation and conquest lusting for power, fame, and fortune:

"There's a lot left of me. Stay tuned!"

"Dolton United" was the theme on May 5 when Mayor Jason House, Clerk Alison Key, and trustees Brittney Norwood, Kiana Belcher and Ed Steave were sworn in before a large audience, many of whom participated handsomely in eradicating Henyard. Aris Montgomery, the pretty, unbowed deputy clerk ridiculed by the Supermayor, had the supreme pleasure of introducing Key. A sense of relief, joy, and vindication permeated the venue as master of ceremonies Dr. Nakita Cloud, a thriving Henyard casualty attired in royal blue like other dignitaries, effusively acknowledged deserving citizens. House exuded calming confidence while pledging to erase the general fund debt in four years. The occasion was undoubtedly sour grapes for trustees Andrew Holmes and Stanley Brown; most assuredly, celebrants did not miss the self-puffing pandemonium perpetrated by Hair Hat Tubman.

Trustee Belcher thanked God and her family when assessing the frenetic four-year journey: "When I came home and cried, when my blood pressure was high, when I just didn't understand what would happen next, they were there. I can call them and say just pray for me."

Kudos went to Sherry Britton, a pioneer in the process whose covert organizing and networking behind the scenes were indispensable.

IamJ9eve says Trustee Holmes, dressed in black rather than blue, is a sellout: "Even your hairline don't want nothin' to do with you."

According to one of her cyber sages, "The Dolton Board will not be completely healed till Brown and Holmes are replaced. They both reek of Tiffany!"

The same week as the transition, and regardless of Henyard's proclamations of Godliness, there was a seismic occasion halfway around the world with locally authentic religious ramifications.

The newest Roman Catholic shrine in America used to be the childhood home of Pope Leo XIV, who was an altar boy at St. Mary of the Assumption church and attended the parish school in Dolton.

"Dolton was very famous for having the worst mayor in America, so it's good that it will be known for something good now," former classmate Sherry Stone said.

A handful of nostalgic Henyard stragglers aside, the tents folded, and the main attraction imploded. The Tiffany A. Henyard circus, its shady sideshows, and the unsavory carnies left the unholy carnage of the township and the village in their wake.

The Lansing Journal, with its finger on the pulse of the Henyard hysteria like no other conventional media outlet, provided balance and professionalism under arduous circumstances, ratifying the importance of community newspapers.

Publisher Melanie Jongsma quoted Jonathan Swift from 1710 accordingly: "Falsehood flies and the truth comes limping after it."

Public knowledge and momentum would not have been feasible without a nucleus of unyielding residents refusing to be discarded. "The light has been shining on the roaches and the roaches scattered," stalwart Dan Lee said.

The ardent activist in the Supermayor saga inspired internet praise: "Jedidiah Brown is the true definition of BOOTS ON THE GROUND... and for those who can't say anything nice...LET'S SEE YOUR BOOTS ON THE GROUND."

The Podcaster Posse tracked Henyard's band of outlaws through the inconceivable, unconscionable, and reprehensible, blending myriad approaches, personalities, and content in their presentations to devout legions of followers from around the nation and beyond.

Sheriff Frank allays the worries of enraptured viewers deriving vicarious joy from Tiffany A. Henyard's narcissism, sociopathy, outrages, and criminality:

"Some people are 'Oh, we gonna have no content to watch.' We can't be happy for content while people are getting robbed by Tiffany Henyard and her entourage. There's always somethin' to cook on. Always."

www.ingramcontent.com/pod-product-compliance
Lightning Source LLC
Chambersburg PA
CBHW052135270326
41930CB00012B/2894